Eng. by W. G. Jackman.

Mrs. HANNAH MORE

HANNAH MORE

OR

Life in Hall and Cottage

BY

Mrs HELEN C. KNIGHT.

BARLEY WOOD THE RESIDENCE OF THE LATE HANNAH MORE.

NEW YORK:

PUBLISHED BY THE AMERICAN TRACT SOCIETY.

HANNAH MORE;

OR,

LIFE IN HALL AND COTTAGE.

BY MRS. HELEN C. KNIGHT.

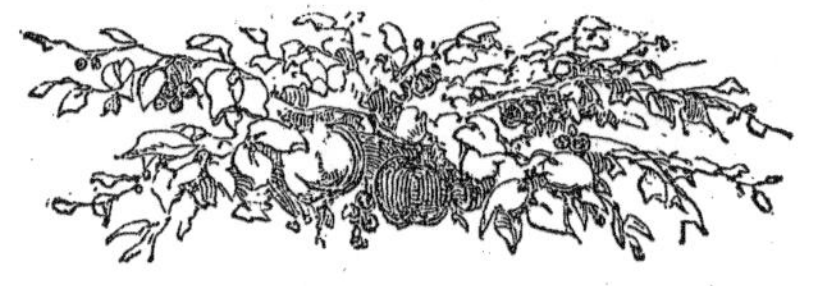

PUBLISHED BY THE
AMERICAN TRACT SOCIETY,
150 NASSAU-STREET, NEW YORK.

CONTENTS.

PREFACE.

It has been written, that "the world's wealth is its original men; by these and their works it is a world and not a waste: the memory and record of what *men* it bore—this is the sum of its strength, its 'sacred property' for ever, whereby it upholds itself and steers forward, better or worse, through the yet undiscovered deep of time.

"Science itself, is it not, under one of its most interesting aspects, biography? Is it not the record of the *work*, which an original man, still named by us or not named, was blessed by the heavens to do?"

May it not also be said that the wealth of the church is her godly men, her holy women, her ransomed little ones? Are not the record and memory of their self-denial and suffering, their patient waiting and cheerful courage, their faith and love, her richest legacies and dearest treasures? By these is the world an Eden, and not a waste; by these is the church the true vine, and not a withered branch; a living epistle, and not a dead letter: the memory and record of what *Christian men* and *women* it bore—this is the sum of her strength, her "sacred property" for ever.

Christianity itself, is it not, under one of its most interesting aspects, *biography?* Is it not the record of the *work* of the GOD-MAN? Have not its doctrines been unfolded by the lives and labors of its eminent disciples?

In this view, what meaning is there in the Christian life, whenever bearing "precious fruit," within the cottage or the hall, in the little child patiently bearing its weary load for Christ's sake, or in those holy and devout ones whose faith subdued kingdoms, wrought righteousness, and who, having obtained a good report, have gone to receive their great recompense of reward.

Herein is the beauty and excellence of the life of this eminent servant of God, HANNAH MORE.

Though among the household memories, if not among the nursery-rhymes of many in middle life, she is less known to a great multitude of the young, who are just entering upon the duties, the responsibilities, and conflicts of the Christian life, and for them is this sketch prepared. If there is a tendency in the church, as some fear, to consult worldly advantages more than Christ's requirements; to be content with a weak faith and feeble hopes, instead of the warm, large, generous love which inspired the apostles of old, and eminent saints of later time; to rest satisfied with only a name to live, instead of bringing forth fruits meet for repentance—let us turn back and study the character of those whose lips and lives most eloquently expressed the holy gospel they professed. Let us inquire what doctrines they believed, what principles they adopted, what duties they discharged, what labors they undertook, what amusements they forsook; in a word, let us seek to find out their apprehension of Bible truth, and how also the Bible shaped their views, moulded their character, and fitted them for usefulness. Hannah More presents one of the most complete models of Christian character; her life is a beautiful development of that healthy, vigorous, life-giving, and heart-warming piety, which springs from the distinguishing doctrines of the Bible cordially believed and faithfully acted upon. Let every American woman study her biography. It is a legacy left for our benefit, a portrait for our contemplation, an example to imitate, a token for encouragement and hope, an earnest of that fulness in Christ Jesus, if we "do show the same diligence to the full assurance of hope unto the end, that we be not slothful, but followers of them who through faith and patience inherit the promises."

This volume, revised from an earlier edition, is now placed among the publications of the American Tract Society.

May its mission be blest.

H. C. K.

A

NEW MEMOIR OF HANNAH MORE.

CHAPTER I.

EARLY DAYS.

LET us visit the retired hamlet of Fishponds; it is in the parish of Stapleton, four miles from Bristol, and possesses all the quiet and homely comfort of rural life in England. Among the humble homes of the hamlet stands that of Mr. Jacob More, a man of piety and learning, who, though bred to larger expectations and an ampler inheritance, is the faithful and contented master of the parish school, the happy husband of his excellent Mary, the proud father of five little girls, and the thankful proprietor of valuable stock in domestic peace and enjoyment. He is a devoted member of the English church, and a loyal subject of "good King George." The overcast fortunes of his early days, and the mansion and estates of Wenhaston wrested from him in a suit at law, are well-nigh forgotten amid the manifold cares and busy interests of family rearing. Besides leading a flock of village urchins to the green pastures of knowledge, he guides his five little girls by the same friendly crook; and in their training he beholds the buds and blossoms, as in their lives he hopes to realize the fruit of his professional skill and parental fidelity.

With more enlarged views of female education than were common a hundred years ago, good Mr. More, though not without a certain horror for a learned lady, determined to strengthen the minds of his daughters by a thorough course of study and well-selected reading: his object was to fit them for usefulness in whatever path the providence of God might direct their steps.

The home influences which surrounded this band of sisters were the purest and best—not harassed by poverty or enervated by luxury, but surrounded by the steady yet gentle pressure of *ever doing*, they were early taught the wonderful power of the "diligent hand;" away from fevered excitements and fashionable follies, they only knew life through the simple habits of their parents, enriched and beautified by the clear sense and devout spirit of their mother, and by the classic tastes and well-stored mind of their father.

As the sisters passed from infancy to childhood, from childhood to womanhood, the daily discipline of reading and grammar, of Latin and mathematics, was diversified and relieved by household labors and rural exercises.

To the studies which fell within Mr. More's own province, he wished to add that of the French language; and for this purpose, when Mary, the eldest, was twelve, she went three times a week to Bristol to receive lessons from the most approved instructors, in order to fit her to become the teacher of her younger sisters. Through hot and cold, through wet and dry, with a resolution which ever afterwards was one of the most prominent traits in her character, Mary More trod unweariedly her solitary four miles' walk, studying with unflinching earnestness until she became a thorough mistress of the French, and spoke it with the fluency and elegance of a native.

While the eldest daughter was thus toiling, Elizabeth, next her in age, was busy by her mother's side plying the needle, turning the wheel, or adding to family comfort through the thousand unseen channels of simple duties and little kindnesses.

Then came Sarah, brimful of wit and humor, whose quaint sayings and lively answers were the delight of her companions, and often provoked a smile from the schoolmaster in his gravest and most thoughtful moods.

Having lost a valuable portion of his library by his unhappy expulsion from the paternal estate, Mr. More was constrained to teach history in the more animated style of conversation and story; and his own interest in Grecian sages and Roman heroes was revived and quickened by the bright eyes and earnest glance of his fourth little one, ever first on her father's knee, listening with a glowing face to the wonderful recitals which fell from his lips. While still regarded as "the little one," and long before she was thought worthy of the paternal teaching, the delighted parents were surprised to find her reading with intelligence and fluency, having slipped through the long apprenticeship of syllables and spelling they hardly knew when or how.

She learned while others talked; a scrap of paper and an old pen are among her baby-house treasures; in rude characters she attempts to put down the thoughts which spring up abundantly within her little bosom. Before her father's door was the high-road leading to Bristol, with its manifold and far off wonders; the child often sits and ponders whence it comes and whither it goes, eagerly watching the heavy carts or the pillion-equestrians as they occasionally pass and repass, each suggesting a new fancy or pleasing wonder. As she ponders, she writes. The little child of four years is a rhymer, perhaps a poet. Besides a poem, her fourth year has other marvels for expectant and loving kindred. The village curate awards her sixpence for catechism lessons well learned and perfectly recited—her first *earned* sixpence. Such were the first laurels of Hannah, the *fourth* child of Mr. More, born in the year 1745.

Her father, delighted with the dawning abilities of the child, soon began to teach her his favorite Latin. Amazed at her rapid progress, he abandoned the work, lest Hannah should grow up a pedant; this however he willingly resumed not long after at the entreaty of the child, seconded by the persuasions of her mother. The little Hannah was henceforth permitted to read, study, and write, as her fancy led; poems, essays, and stories issued from her pen, and were stored away to be read or recited to her sisters, whose sympathy encouraged her endeavors.

Patty was the youngest of the flock, loving and joyous, never jealous of the opening powers of her sister, for whom her admiration was only equalled by her affection.

As the family grew up, its increasing wants outran its straitened means, when the elder sisters proposed to follow the profession of their father, and try the experiment of a new boarding-school in the neighboring city.

Warm friends, who knew their worth, seconded the plan, and offered their patronage and influence. Among their patrons was Mrs. Gwatkin, a lady of worth and high position, who then little dreamed that, through the friendly aid she rendered to this band of teachers, her own name should be handed to generations yet to come. The family circle was broken up. Mary, Elizabeth, and Sarah left the paternal roof to try their fortunes in the great world: the school opened, scholars flocked to it, and the first year confirmed their hopes and encouraged farther efforts. With what solicitude and pride must the father have watched their progress in the same ordeal of daily struggles, in which he had already become a veteran; and when at last, at the age of twelve, he suffered the little Hannah to escape from his nest and become a pupil in the now prosperous school, he gave the strongest proof which a father could give of his confidence in the well-conducted enterprise.

A world of interest opened upon the gifted girl in the wider sphere of study and observation, in the diversity of character, in the new friendships and associations, in the competitions and struggles of school-life in the city. She was not among strangers who, caring not, crowded her mind or cramped her heart; affection still folded her in its bosom, defending her from harmful flatteries, yet rejoicing in her opening and maturing powers. Her progress was brilliant and rapid, reflecting honor upon the school, and attracting attention from some of the most cultivated minds in the city. Sir James Stonehouse, a friend and patron of her sisters, whose writings for the spiritual benefit of the sick have been extensively circulated by the Society for Promoting Christian Knowledge, took every opportunity of cultivating the young girl's friendship, and while she was yet a pupil predicted her distinguished career.

Besides Sir James, Dr. Tucker, afterwards dean of Gloucestershire, Mr. Peach, a man of extensive reading and fine taste, and Ferguson the astronomer, then lecturing at Bristol, sought her society with delight, and were reckoned among her warmest friends. So great, at that early period, were the charms of her conversation, that Dr. Woodward, her physician, a man of some eminence in his time, is said one day altogether to have forgotten his professional duty in listening, until half way down stairs, suddenly recollecting himself, he exclaimed, "Bless me, I forgot to ask the girl how she was," and hastened back to amend the delinquency.

Hannah's literary tastes showed themselves in her pastimes as well as in her studies, for we learn that a favorite diversion was the gathering of small parties, where the talk was wholly sustained in the language of Shakspeare, and "it was surprising," she said in after-days, "how well the conversation was kept up." It must be remembered that children's literature had then no existence; the Parent's Assistant, Sanford and Merton, Harry and Lucy, books which a few years afterwards delighted the young, had not then appeared. Children read then, if they read at all, books which their elders read and loved, and Shakspeare, it seems, was among the select reading of young Hannah More. This early appreciation of his writings imparted to one of her first journeys a zest and enjoyment which few at her age could have been supposed to feel.

In company with friends she visited Stratford-upon-the-Avon, the birthplace of the immortal poet, and brought away a branch of the famous mulberry growing in his garden; this she had wrought into sugar-tongs and presented to Mrs. Gwatkin, with the verse,

"I kissed the sacred shrine where Shakspeare lay,
And bore this relic of my bard away:
Where shall I place it, Phœbus? Where 't is due,
Apollo answered: and I send it—*you.*"

At seventeen a small work issued from her pen, entitled, "The Search after Happiness," a pastoral drama, which, with an ever-grateful sense of Mrs. Gwatkin's kindness to her family, she dedicated to that lady.

Unexpected success crowned the efforts of the sisters: their faithful and judicious management of the home department, together with the superior course of instruction given in the school, gave it a deservedly high position, and attracted pupils from the most distant parts of the kingdom. The sisters determined to enlarge their boundaries, and for this purpose they built a large and commodious house in Park-street, where the number of applicants still outrun their accommodations.

Nor were they unmindful of the comfort and increasing infirmities of their now only remaining parent. Mr. More, bereft of his family, was moved to a pleasant house in the city, where he passed a green old age in the enjoyment of his garden, his library, his friends, and above all, the daily visits of his five excellent daughters.

Having completed her studies, Hannah remained in the school as teacher. Beloved and respected in no common degree, the younger sisters were often invited to visit the homes of their pupils. They were at this time intimate with two young ladies, who frequently carried them to Belmont, the residence of a cousin, Edward Turner, Esq., six miles from Bristol. Hannah's fine taste and cultivated mind made a strong impression on the host, who delighted to consult her about his projected improvements, and followed her suggestions in many of the embellishments made on his estate.

It is no surprise that she won his affection, and for a time at least wooed him from his love of single life. Though twice her age—Hannah was now nearly twenty-two—he sought her hand; the suit was favorably regarded, and the bridal preliminaries were completed, when the current of true love, not always smoothly running, drifted them apart; nor does it appear that Hannah ever afterwards freighted her bark on the same uncertain element.

Mr. Turner never ceased to regard her with respect and interest, and his first toast every day, whether alone or in society, was "Hannah More." In after-years, their long-suspended intercourse was renewed, and continued until his death, when he bequeathed to her a thousand pounds. There are no regrets to bestow over this severed tie, for Mrs. Turner might have deprived the world of the brilliant career and valuable services of Miss Hannah More. She afterwards received an offer of marriage from Dr. Langhorne, vicar of Blagdon, a man of lively wit and cultivated intellect, with whom she became acquainted while in quest of health and strength on the coast of Somersetshire. Behold her on the beach, sometimes on a pillion behind her servant, sometimes in company with the doctor, sometimes surrounded by a group of admiring friends, drawn thither by the charms of her brilliant and animated conversation. Though a rejected suitor, the doctor maintained a poetical and literary correspondence with the lady until his death, which took place in the prime of a manhood blighted by irregularities and misfortune.

Thus far have we caught passing glimpses of Hannah More in the dear seclusion of her early home, the busy retreat of her sisters' school, and the agreeable circle of Bristol society, where her simple manners, her good sense, and the unaffected friendliness of her heart, gave an added lustre to those brilliant powers and that ready wit which afterwards made her a welcome and honored guest in the elegant and refined circles of the metropolis. How much is there in her early life of which the few and scanty records that remain fail to inform us! How many an earnest mother would rend the veil which conceals her childhood, to learn the secret springs of that Christian nurture which enabled her to pass unseduced and unscathed through the trying ordeal of folly, of fashion, and of fame which awaited her. The glitter of fashionable life never seems to have dimmed the clearness of her moral vision, or prevented her from making a rational estimate of its maxims, habits, and pursuits; there ever accompanied her an integrity of moral consciousness, a hidden strength, which, stronger than breastplate or shield, defended her from the corrupting influence of flattery, and enabled her to maintain that singleness and purity of character, and to foster those religious convictions which formed the beauty and excellence of her riper years.

CHAPTER II.

INTRODUCTION TO LONDON SOCIETY.

BRILLIANT minds centre round this period of English literature. The splendid diction of Burke had kindled a fresh glow around "The Sublime and Beautiful;" the Deserted Village was peopled with admirers; Johnson enriched the world of letters from the storehouse of his affluent mind; Sir Joshua Reynolds was in the zenith of his popularity; and Garrick ruled the stage.

London society was rife with genius, wit, and learning; the famous Blue Stocking Club was then in its glory, and its accomplished patrons figured in the most elegant and refined circles of that day. This gathering, which has unwittingly given a name of implied reproach to women of literary tastes and pursuits, was composed of persons distinguished for wit and talent, who met at each other's houses to enjoy the charm of each other's society, without ceremony or supper, and without the interloping aid of cards or dancing, as we learn from a little poem entitled the Bas Bleu, written by Hannah More a few years after.

> "Long was society o'errun
> By Whist, that desecrating Hun;
> Long did Quadrille despotic sit,
> That Vandal of colloquial wit,
> And conversation's setting light
> Lay deep obscured in Gothic night:
> At length the mental shades decline;
> Colloquial wit begins to shine;
> Genius prevails, and conversation
> Emerges into reformation."

Among the admired women of this circle ranks Mrs. Elizabeth Montagu, who acquired much celebrity as the author of an "Essay on the Genius of Shakspeare," published in 1769. She became better known in this country by a volume of delightful letters, which charmed the reading world fifty years ago. Beautiful in youth, and left in possession of an ample fortune at the death of her husband, she retained until the latest period of life a grace of person and manner, which made her splendid mansion at Berkeley-square a centre of the most polished society in the metropolis. By her side sits Elizabeth Carter, accounted one of the most learned ladies of her time, the long-loved and intimate companion of Mrs. Montagu. At twenty-nine, Dr. Johnson, in a fit of unusual gallantry, composed a Greek epigram to her praise; and she was almost the only lady, through long years of intercourse, whom he treated with uniform attention and civility. For the encouragement of the young, who are more ready to question their abilities than to exercise them, and for the benefit of teachers impatient of progress which they are not faithful enough to secure, let it be added that Mr. Carter, in early days Elizabeth's instructor, became so disgusted by the apparent stupidity of his daughter, that he abandoned the task of teaching her; while she, with a resolution which nothing could quench, continued her studies until she became one of the most thorough scholars of her sex. Dr. Johnson, speaking of a celebrated Greek scholar, said he understood Greek better than anybody else, except Elizabeth Carter; and the fishermen of Deal, her native place, respectfully regarded her as the *almanac maker*, that being the highest conception they could form of the abilities and power of their distinguished townswoman. Her biography may be found in some of our older libraries, together with "Mrs. Chapone's Letters to Young Ladies," a famous book in its day, whose wise counsel and judicious guidance no young lady could presume to be without.

Here is Mrs. Chapone, one of the Blue Stockings, with another no less distinguished, Hon. Frances Boscawen, widow of Admiral Boscawen, a warm and appreciating friend of literary worth and rising genius. With her comes Mrs. Vesey, to whom, in pleasing remembrance of the delightful gatherings at her house, Miss More dedicated her Bas Bleu poem,

"Vesey, of sense the judge and friend."

Brilliant as these circles were, they were yet to receive a delightful accession in the gifted woman, who, in company with her sister Sarah, left Bristol on a visit to London in the winter of 1773, and began, as she says, for the first time, to "know something of the hurry, bustle, dissipation, and nonsensical flutter of town life."

Her reputation had already preceded her, and Hannah More is soon a guest at the table of Sir Joshua Reynolds, whose handsome establishment in Leicester-fields was the resort of the gay and learned. Hosts of friends surrounded his board, drawn thither as much by his genial hospitality as by the world-wide reputation of his genius, and the monuments of his industry and art. His sister Frances, with whom Hannah was soon intimate, presided over his house. Miss Reynolds, if we may credit a contemporary critic, seems not to have been a very skilful housewife, or to have served her brother's table with an especial reference to order or arrangement, there often being a deficiency of knives, forks, plates, and glasses; yet friends long loved the memory of those social gatherings, which, after the sun had set that gave them warmth, no one ever attempted to revive or imitate.

We next follow her to Hampton Court, the princely domain of Cardinal Woolsey, sixteen miles from London. Here were royal halls, with their superb pictures and ancient tapestry; the beauties of King William's court, looking beautiful still through the stiff and antique drapery of elder times; and the records of royal industry, tapestry wrought by Queen Mary's hands, when, surrounded by her maidens, "the needle plied its busy task."

Not far off were the "immortal shades" of Twickenham, the abode of Pope, one of her favorite authors, only a pleasant walk's distance from Hampton Court. The curious domain of the poet, at that time in possession of Sir William Stanhope, had suffered few outward changes; the rooms had been stripped of every memento of its former occupant: his bust, statue, pictures, and library, many of them gifts of distinguished men, and tributes to his genius, had been scattered far and wide among his friends; but the house remained, with its curiously wrought arcades, columns, and porticos. The garden, shrubbery, and grotto were also there, where Addison, Swift, Parnel, and Bolingbroke "read, wrought, and wrote," far away from the busy and distracting scenes of London life; nor could she leave without plucking a sprig of laurel from the garden, and stealing two stones from the grotto, in memory of the great departed: neither did she leave Twickenham without visiting his tomb in the village churchyard bearing the inscription, "One who would not be buried in Westminster Abbey," he, as Hannah wittily suggested, probably choosing to be the first ghost in Twickenham rather than an inferior one at Westminster.

On her return to Hampton, she went to the country house of David Garrick, beautifully situated on the Thames, then undergoing repairs. She wandered over the grounds, and stole into his temple, a quiet garden retreat, containing, among other things, a chair curiously wrought from the tree which grew in Shakspeare's garden.

"I sat in it," wrote she to Mrs. Gwatkin, "but caught no inspiration. What drew my attention most was a splendid statue of that great and original man, in an attitude strikingly pensive; his limbs strongly muscular, his countenance expressive of some vast conception, and his whole form seeming the bigger from some immense idea, with which you suppose his imagination pregnant. The statue cost £500."

The drama was then a favorite with Hannah More: her first article was dramatic, and she had already sketched some of the thrilling scenes in Hebrew history, which afterwards appeared in the form of "Sacred Dramas." No wonder that Garrick was at once an object of curiosity and interest. It was in the character of King Lear that she first beheld his remarkable powers, a graphic description of which in a letter to a mutual friend inspired him with the strongest desire to see and know her. Though somewhat past the prime of life, having nearly reached his sixtieth year, Garrick's frame still retained the flexibility and vigor of earlier days. With genius and refinement, "the finest man in the world for sprightly conversation," as Johnson tells us, his house, adorned by Eva Maria his beautiful and accomplished wife, was a centre of attraction to the literary circles of that period.

An introduction soon followed: the interview gave mutual pleasure, and the foundations of a warm and cordial intimacy were laid, which lasted until his death. Garrick immediately introduced his new friend into the elegant circle over which Mrs. Montagu presided: she soon became a frequent guest at Berkeley-square, and a favorite of the choice spirits of that day.

But Hannah longed to behold the wonder of the age, "Irene Johnson!" "Dictionary Johnson!" "Idler, Rambler Johnson!" Calling one day at Sir Joshua's, she learned he was within: her friends tried to moderate her eagerness by hinting at the rudeness of his manners. On entering the room, she was agreeably surprised by a cordial greeting in a verse of her own poetry and a condescending advance to receive her. Sir Joshua's macaw was jauntily perched on his arm, a favorite of the doctor for its appreciating estimate of young Northcote's work—a portrait of one of the servants, whom the bird mistaking for the original, against which it harbored a grudge, flew at it with the greatest fury, and nearly picked the canvas to pieces.

Hannah was favorably impressed, and not long afterwards, in company with Miss Reynolds, she paid Dr. Johnson a visit at his own lodgings. On entering his little parlor, they found it occupied by a pale, shrunken old lady, dressed in scarlet, her head covered by a black lace hood with stiff projecting wings. Jumping into a great armchair, which she naturally concluded could be nobody's accustomed seat but the doctor's, Hannah playfully invoked the inspiration of his genius.

Their hostess was Miss Anna Williams, the blind poetess, who for forty years was sheltered beneath the doctor's roof. The daughter of an early friend, on coming up to London, before his wife's death, for the purpose of having an operation performed upon her eyes, she was invited to his house. Failing in the expected aid, Dr. Johnson offered her a home.

Her destitute situation enlisted the sympathy of his friends, and she received from them substantial support. Garrick gave her a benefit, Mrs. Montagu allowed her ten pounds a year, and Miss Carter electioneered a long subscription for her poems.

The heavy tread of the host is at the door: he enters: behold his burly and unwieldy body, with face disfigured by scrofula, and head surmounted by a large, bushy, grayish wig, well singed, or perhaps quite crisp in front—a fright to the respectable company of wigs with which it daily associates: its master's eyes are both weak and near-sighted, and in his absorbing interest for a favorite author, he often brings them in dangerous proximity to the light, quite regardless of consequences. On his dining with distinguished guests at Leicester-fields, Sir Joshua's butler used to take the liberty of replacing the old wig with one more suitable to the dignity of the occasion.

He is dressed in plain brown clothes, black worsted stockings, and silver knee-buckles. His rolling gait, with the odd and convulsive twists of his unwieldy body, added to a harsh and imperious voice, were sufficiently disagreeable to repulse the least fastidious.

At the time of Hannah's introduction to him, he was past sixty-five, bearing the accumulated infirmities of age and disease, yet keenly alive as ever to the pleasures of conversation and tea. No person probably enjoyed more the cup which "cheers but not inebriates," or possessed a more appreciative sense of the qualities of Bohea.

Come early or late, the tea-table was sure to be spread. By the friendly inspiration of the fragrant leaf, his morning was endured, his evenings solaced; and he could talk the twenty-four hours together without weariness or rest, if a considerate regard to the bed-time of his friends did not occasionally release them from his company.

"I lie down," he once said, "that my acquaintance may sleep; for I lie down to endure oppressive misery, and soon rise again to pass the night in anxiety and pain." Poor Johnson's bodily existence was a torture.

As he enters the little parlor in Fleet-street, the callers are cordially received; he laughs heartily at Hannah, and disowns all special occupancy of the armchair in which she sits.

Perhaps they discuss his "Journey to the

Hebrides," just published, a work investing the dryest subject with interest, and turning a most barren spot to profitable account, four thousand copies of the work having been sold the first week of its publication.

On Hannah's return to Bristol, in 1774, her feelings became warmly enlisted for her favorite candidate in the Parliament election then going on, Hon. Edmund Burke, who made the friendship, and was a frequent guest of the Misses More. When his success at the polls became certain, the sisters presented him their congratulatory addresses, through a splendid cockade, composed of "the sublime and beautiful" colors analyzed in his famous essay, twined with myrtle, decorated with silver tassels, and filled with appropriate mottoes. The box was handed him in a large party; and being opened, the cockade was taken out amid the applauses of his friends and a general curiosity concerning the giver. Burke declared it could only be from the Park-street sisters. It was elevated to a conspicuous situation in the committee-room, and graced his cap on the day of his triumph.

CHAPTER III.

A PEEP AT THE BLUES.

THE bright world of intellectual life and social elegance into which Hannah More was suddenly and unexpectedly ushered, while it brought her into the society of people whom it was a pleasure and a privilege to know, also brought her into contact with amusements and habits not only foreign to her tastes, but opposed to her principles. In her free home letters, full of good sense and graphic description, she opens a loophole into her heart and habits.

The following was written during her second visit to London, in 1775:

"Our visit was at Sir Joshua's, where we were received with all the friendship imaginable. I am going to-day to a great dinner: nothing can be conceived so absurd, extravagant, and fantastical, as the present mode of dressing the head. Simplicity and modesty are things so much exploded, that their very names are no longer remembered. I have just escaped from one of the fashionable disfigurers; and though I charged him to dress me with the greatest simplicity, and to have only a very distant eye upon the fashion, just enough to avoid the pride of singularity, yet in spite of all these sage cautions, I absolutely blush at myself, and turn to the glass with as much caution as a vain beauty just risen from the small-pox, which cannot be a more disfiguring disease than the present mode of dress. Of the one, the calamity may be greater in its consequences; but of the other, it is more corrupt in its cause.

"We have been reading a treatise on the morality of Shakspeare. It is a happy and easy way of filling a book that the present race of authors have arrived at—that of criticizing the works of some eminent poet, with monstrous extracts and short remarks. It is a species of cookery that I begin to grow tired of: they cut up their authors in chops, and by adding a little crumbled bread of their own, and tossing it up a little, they present it as a fresh dish: you are to dine upon the poet; the critic supplies the garnish, yet has the credit as well as the profit of the whole entertainment."

"London, 1775.

"I had yesterday the pleasure of dining in Hill-street, Berkeley-square, at a certain Mrs. Montagu's, a name not totally obscure. The party consisted of herself, Mrs. Carter, Dr. Johnson, Salander, and Matty, Mrs. Boscawen, Miss Reynolds, and Sir Joshua—the idol of every company—some other persons of high rank and less wit, and your humble servant, a party that would not have disgraced the table of Lelius or of Atticus. I felt myself a worm, the more a worm for the consequence which was given me by mixing me with such a society; but as I told Mrs. Boscawen, and with great truth, I had an opportunity of making an experiment of my heart, by which I learned that I was not envious, for I certainly did not repine at being the meanest person in company.

"Mrs. Montagu received me with the most encouraging kindness; she is not only the finest genius, but the finest lady I ever saw. She lives in the highest style of magnificence; her apartments and table are in the most splendid taste: but what baubles are these when speak- of a Montagu! Her form—for she has no *body*—is delicate even to fragility; her countenance the most animated in the world; the sprightly vivacity of fifteen with the judgment and experience of a Nestor. But I fear she is hastening to decay very fast. Her spirits are so active that they must soon wear out the little frail receptacle that holds them. Mrs. Carter has in her person a great deal of what the gentlemen mean when they say such a one is a 'poetical lady.' However, independently of her great talents and learning, I like her much: she has affability, kindness, and goodness, and I honor her heart even more than her talents. But I do not like one of them better than Mrs. Boscawen: she is at once polite, learned, judicious, and humble; and Mrs. Palk tells me her letters are not thought inferior to Mrs. Montagu's. She regretted—so did I—that so many suns could not possibly shine at one time: but we are to have a smaller party, where from fewer luminaries there may emanate a clearer, steadier, and more beneficial light. Dr. Johnson asked me how I liked the new tragedy of Braganze. I was afraid to speak before company: however, as I thought it a less evil to dissent from the opinion of a fellow-creature than to tell a falsity, I ventured to give my sentiments, and was satisfied with

Johnson's answering, 'You are right, madam.'"

With sisterly pride, and in a tone of affectionate eulogy, Sarah, who joined Hannah in her winter sojourning at London, thus writes, in her bright and lively style, to the sisterhood at Bristol:

"London, 1775.

"Tuesday evening we drank tea at Sir Joshua's, with Dr. Johnson. Hannah is certainly a great favorite. She was placed next him, and they had the entire conversation to themselves. They were both in remarkably high spirits: it was certainly her lucky night. I never heard her say so many good things. The old genius was extremely jocular, and the young one very pleasant. You would have imagined we had been at some comedy, had you heard our peals of laughter. They indeed tried which could 'pepper the highest,' and it is not clear to me that the lexicographer was really the highest seasoner. Yesterday, Mr. Garrick called upon us; a volume of Pope lay upon the table: we asked him to read, and he went through the latter part of the 'Essay on Man.' He was exceedingly good-humored, and expressed himself quite delighted with our eager desire for information; and when he had satisfied our interrogatory, 'Now, madam, what next?' He read several lines we had been disputing about, with regard to emphasis, in many different ways, before he decided which was right. He sat with us from half-past twelve till three, reading and criticizing. We have just had a call from Mr. Burke."

"LONDON, 1775.

"'Bear me, some god, O quickly bear me hence,
To wholesome solitude, the nurse of—'

'Sense,' I was going to add, in the words of Pope, till I recollected that *pence* had a more appropriate meaning, and was as good a rhyme. This apostrophe broke from me," writes Hannah, "on coming from the opera, the first I ever *did*, the last, I trust, I ever *shall* go to. For what purpose has the Lord of the universe made his creature man with a comprehensive mind? why make him a little lower than the angels? why give him the faculty of thinking, the powers of wit and memory, and to crown all, an immortal and never-dying spirit? Why all this wondrous waste, this prodigality of bounty, if the mere animal senses of sight and hearing—by which he is not distinguished from the brutes that perish—would have answered the end as well? and yet I find that the same people are seen at the opera every night, an amusement written in a language the greater part of them do not understand, and performed by such a set of beings. But the man

> 'Who bade the reign commence
> Of rescued nature and reviving sense,'

sat at my elbow, and reconciled me to my situation, not by his approbation, but his presence. Going to the opera, like getting drunk, is a sin that carries its own punishment with it, and that a very severe one. Thank my dear Dr. Stonehouse for his kind and seasonable admonitions on my last Sunday's engagement at Mrs. Montagu's. Conscience had done its office before; nay, was busy at the time; and if it did not dash the cup of pleasure to the ground, infused at least a tincture of wormwood into it. I *did* think of the alarming call, 'What doest thou here, Elijah?' and I thought of it to-night at the opera."

"Sunday night, 9 o'clock.

"Perhaps you will say I ought to have thought of it again to-day, when I tell you I have dined abroad; but it is a day I reflect on without those uneasy sensations one has when one is conscious it has been spent in trifling company. I have been at Mrs. Boscawen's. Mrs. Montagu, Mrs. Carter, Mrs. Chapone, and myself only were admitted. We spent the time, not as wits, but as reasonable creatures; better characters, I trow. The conversation was sprightly, but serious. I have not enjoyed an afternoon so much since I have been in town. There was much sterling sense, and they are all ladies of high character for piety, of which, however, I do not think their visiting on Sunday any proof; for though their conversation is edifying, the example is bad.

"The more I see of the 'honored, famed, and great,' the more I see of the littleness, the unsatisfactoriness of all created good, and that no earthly pleasure can fill up the wants of the immortal principle within. One need go no farther than the company I have just left, to be convinced that 'pain is for man,' and that fortune, talents, and science, are no exemption from the universal lot. Mrs. Montagu, eminently distinguished for wit and virtue, 'the wisest where all are wise,' is hastening to insensible decay by a slow but sure hectic. Mrs. Chapone has experienced the severest reverses of fortune; and Mrs. Boscawen's life has been a continued series of afflictions, that may almost bear a parallel with those of the righteous man of Uz. Tell me, then, what is it to be wise? This, you will say, is exhibiting the unfavorable side of the picture of humanity; but it is the right side, the side that shows the likeness."

CHAPTER IV.

LITERARY BLOSSOMINGS.

While Miss More was at home in the winter of 1775, she one day said to her sisters, "I have been so fed with praise, I think I will venture to try what my real value is, by writing a slight poem."

Her social position was much changed since the Pastoral Drama issued from her pen at the desk of the noisy school-room, beyond which her fame and influence were but just extending.

Within a fortnight two poems were completed, "Sir Eldred of the Bower," and "The Bleeding Rock." These, on her return to London, she presented to a well-known publisher, Cadell, who offered her forty guineas, promising at the same time, could she discover what Goldsmith received for his "Deserted Village," to increase the sum to that amount.

Of this flattering award of pounds and pence, the "Deserted Village" has now no right to feel envious, for it has a perpetual inheritance in our hearts, while "Sir Eldred," after a brief patronage from the great men of his day, has passed into obscurity and neglect.

Miss Sally More, who accompanied Hannah to London, writes home the gratifying news: "From Miss Reynolds we learn that Sir Eldred is the theme of conversation in all the polite circles, and that the beauteous Bertha has kindled a flame in the cold heart of Johnson, who declares that her parent has but one fault, which is, suffering herself to graze upon the barren rocks of Bristol, while the rich pastures of London are guarded by no fence which could exclude her from them."

In another letter she adds, "If a wedding should take place before our return, do n't be surprised—between the mother of Sir Eldred and the father of Irene; nay, Mrs. Montagu says, if tender words are the precursors of connubial engagements, we may expect great things; for it is nothing but 'child,' 'a little fool,' 'love,' and 'dearest.' After much critical discourse, he turns round to me, and with one of his most amiable looks, which must be seen to form the least idea of, he says, 'I have heard you are engaged in the useful and honorable occupation of teaching young ladies;' upon which, with all the ease, familiarity, and confidence we should have done had only our dear Dr. Stonehouse been present, we entered upon the history of our birth, parentage, and education, showing how we were born with more desires than guineas, and how as years increased our appetites, the cupboard at length began to grow too small for them, and how with a bottle of water, a bed and a blanket, we set out to seek our fortunes; and how we found a great house with nothing in it; and how it was like to remain so, till, looking into our knowledge-boxes, we happened to find a little learning a very good thing when land is gone; and so at last, by giving a little of this to those who had less, we got a good store of gold in return; but how, alas, we wanted the wit to keep it. 'I love you both,' cried the doctor. 'I love you all five. I never was at Bristol; I will come on purpose to see you. What, five women live happily together! I will come and see you. I have spent a happy evening; I am glad I came; God for ever keep you; you live to shame duchesses.' He took his leave with so much warmth and tenderness we were quite affected by his manner."

The sisters visited Garrick at his pleasant rural home at Hampton, where he entertained them by reading a whimsical correspondence in prose and verse, carried on for many years with the first geniuses of that age.

"We see him now," says Patty, "in his mellower light, when the world has been shaken off. He says he longs to enter into himself, and to study the more important duties of life, which he is determined upon doing. The next time we go, Hannah is to carry some of her writing; she is to have a little table by herself, and to continue her studies, while he does the same."

"I dined at the Adelphi yesterday," writes Hannah, in one of her letters home, revealing just what we want to know. "It was a particular occasion, an annual meeting, where nothing but men are usually asked. I, however, was of the party, and an agreeable day it was to me. I have seldom heard so much wit under the banner of so much decorum. Colman and Dr. Schomburg were of the party; the rest were chiefly old doctors of divinity. At six I begged leave to come home, as I expected a polite assembly a little after seven. They came at seven. The dramatis personæ were Mrs. Boscawen,

Mrs. Garrick, and Miss Reynolds: my beaux were Dr. Johnson, Dean Tucker, and last, but not least in our love, David Garrick. You know that wherever Johnson is, the confinement to the tea-table is rather a durable situation, and it was an hour and a half before I got my enlargement. Garrick was the very soul of the company, and I never saw Johnson in such perfect good-humor. Sally knows that we have often heard that one can never properly enjoy the company of these two unless they are together. There is great truth in this remark; for after the dean and Mrs. Boscawen—who were the only strangers—were withdrawn, and the rest stood up to go, Johnson and Garrick began a close encounter, telling old stories, 'e'en from their boyish days,' at Litchfield. We all stood around them for above an hour, laughing in defiance of every rule of Chesterfield. Johnson outstaid them all, and sat with me half an hour."

At the repeated solicitations of the Garricks, Miss More soon after took up her abode at the Adelphi, their town house, of which she humorously says, "The master and mistress are sensible, well-behaved people, and keep good company; besides, they are fond of books, and can read, and have a shelf full, which they lend me. Add to this, it is not a common lodging-house: they are careful whom they take in, and will have no people of bad character, or who keep irregular hours.

"I have a great deal of time at my own disposal, to read my own books and see my own friends; and whenever I please, may join in the most elegant and polished society in the world. Our breakfasts are little literary societies; there is generally company at meals, as they think it saves time, by avoiding the necessity of seeing people at other seasons. Mr. Garrick sets the highest value upon his time. I detest and avoid public places more than ever, and should make a miserably bad fine lady."

Some idea may be formed of her industry, that among all this social attraction, she could find time to read four or five hours every day, and sometimes write ten.

There is something heart-warming in the cordial and unfettered intercourse of Hannah and her London friends. The circle contained almost every element for social enjoyment: none indeed has been more famed for colloquial powers, to which wit, learning, and refinement, good-breeding, good-nature, and good-sense, made generous contributions.

Miss More once said to Horace Walpole, that "the truest objects of warm attachment are the small parts of great characters." Who does not love Cowper taming his hares, or enjoy Johnson sipping his tea, or Pope at work in his garden, when the talents which inspired our admiration, and seemed to lift their possessor beyond the common reach of our sympathies, take pleasure in those slender joys which make up the sum of common happiness?

"Let me tell you a ridiculous circumstance which happened the other day," writes Hannah in one of her delightful home-letters. "After dinner Garrick took up the Monthly Review—civil gentlemen, by the by, these monthly reviewers—and read 'Sir Eldred' with all his grace and pathos. I think I was never so ashamed in my life; but he read it so superlatively that I cried like a child. Only think, what a scandalous thing to cry at the reading of one's own poetry! I could have beaten myself; for it looked as if I thought it very moving, which I can truly say is far from being the case. But the beauty of the jest lies in this: Mrs. Garrick twinkled as well as I, and made as many apologies for crying at her husband's reading, as I did for crying at my own verses. *She* got out of the scrape by pretending that she was touched by the story, and *I* by saying the same thing of the reading. It furnished us a great laugh at the catastrophe, when it really would have been decent to have been a little more sorrowful."

Garrick, for so many years the pride of the English stage, was now about to quit it for the calm of private life. Having nearly reached his "chair age," and becoming increasingly subject to severe attacks of sickness, he resolved to leave with all his honors thick upon him. Before doing so, he consented once more, and for the last time, to exhibit his remarkable powers, and for two or three weeks Drury Lane was filled with admiring audiences. In the character of Hamlet, Garrick is said to have excelled—filling, with singular power, says one, the whole soul of the spectator, and transcending the most finished idea of the poet.

"I have at last," writes Hannah on this occasion to Dr. Stonehouse, "had the entire satisfaction of seeing Garrick in Hamlet. Posterity will never be able to form the slightest idea of his powers. The more I see him, the more I wonder and admire. It seems to me as if I had been assisting at the funeral obsequies of the poets. I feel almost as much pain as pleasure. He is quite happy in the prospect of his release."

The strong intelligence of his eye, the animated and ever-varying expression of his whole countenance, the flexibility of his voice, with his grace and ease of attitude, is said altogether to have produced an indescribable and profound impression upon the mind, and one which no language can convey to another.

At the final parting Garrick wept, while tears and applauses accompanied him from the stage. This occurred in May, 1776.

He soon afterwards disposed of his share in Drury Lane for £35,000, and retreated to domestic privacy. Touching the event, Hannah expressed herself in the concluding verses of a little poem, written after her return to Bristol, and addressed to Dragon, Garrick's favorite dog.

"How wise, long pampered with applause,
To make a voluntary pause,
And lay his laurels down!
Boldly repelling each strong claim,
To dare assert to wealth and fame,
Enough of both I've known.

How wise, a short retreat to steal,
The vanity of life to feel,
And from its cares to fly:
To act one calm, domestic scene,
Earth's bustle and the grave between,
Retire, and learn to die."

What Dragon failed to appreciate, the poet naturally concluded his master would. Manuscript copies were handed around and read by her friends, until she was induced to publish it in 1778, when a thousand copies were sold in a single week.

On the following summer we find Miss More journeying into Norfolk, hunting up old friends of her father, visiting country cousins, eating brown bread and custards, and thoroughly appreciating all the good-sense which fell in her way.

Hannah never knew whether to be angry or ashamed, whether to scold or to blush at the fashionable impositions of her day. "I protest," she exclaimed, in speaking of some young ladies who came in to pay her an evening's visit, "I hardly do them justice when I pronounce that they had among them, on their heads, an acre and a half of shrubbery, besides slopes, grass-plats, tulip-beds, clumps of peonies, kitchen-gardens, and green-houses."

"Some ladies carry on their heads a large quantity of fruit, and yet they would despise a poor, useful member of society who carried it there for the purpose of selling it for bread. Spirit of Addison," she humorously supplicates, "thou, who with such fine humor and polished sarcasm didst lash the cherry-colored hood and party patches, and cut down a whole harvest of follies, awake; for the follies thou didst lash were but the beginning of follies, and the absurdities thou didst censure were but the seeds of absurdities."

Garrick, it is said, struck the first blow to this fashionable folly, by appearing one evening on the stage, his cap decorated with a profusion of every sort of vegetable, with a huge carrot hanging down on either side.

One cannot help thinking that the spirit of reform has been heard in the councils of fashion, for her sway is surely more benign in our own day; indeed, when we compare the frightful wigs and cushions, the high-heeled shoes and buckram bodices of our grandames, with the comparative ease and naturalness of our own times, one cannot help hoping that Fashion has entered into a league of good-fellowship with Nature, graciously allowing her the exercise of some of her inalienable rights to life and liberty, if not to the pursuit of happiness.

But if the follies of London, aped in the retreats of Hertfordshire, pained and provoked her, she found some amends in a visit to Mrs. Barbauld, and in the sterling merits of her cousin Cotton, from whose style of living she draws the following sensible conclusion, true all the world over, and worthy the serious consideration of people whose expenses are getting the better of their principles and their purses. "I have long ago found out that hardly anybody but frugal, plain people do generous things. Our cousin Cotton, who I dare say is often ridiculed for his simplicity and frugality, could yet lay down £200, without being sure of ever receiving a shilling interest, for the laudable purpose of establishing a worthy minister, to whom he is still a very considerable contributor. This is commonly the case; and I am apt to conceive a prejudice against everybody who makes a great figure, and to suspect those who *talk* generously."

On her return, she accompanied the Garricks to Farnborough-place, the residence of Mr. Wilmot, where she met, among other distinguished guests, Dr. Kennicott, Hebrew Professor of Oxford, and his wife, with whom Miss More formed a life-long friendship.

In the year 1777, at the urgent entreaty of Garrick, she determined to try her powers for the stage, and "Percy" was the fruit of her labors. Delighted with her success, he recommended it to Mr. Harris the manager of Drury Lane. The tragedy was accepted, and preparations were speedily made for bringing it out. Hannah went to London to bespeak a prologue from Garrick, who humorously begged to know what she meant to pay him; Dryden, he declared, used to have five guineas; but as he was a richer man, he would be content with a handsome supper. The author insisted she could only afford a beef-steak and a bottle of porter. At last they settled down on toast and honey—highly flavored, we may venture to add, with wit and good-humor.

Percy was received with acclamation, and for twelve nights was played to overflowing houses, netting her £700.

The Duke of Northumberland and the Earl of Percy sent to congratulate her on her great success, and to thank her for the honor she had done them by selecting her subject from the historical records of their family. Detained at home by the gout, they sent and bought tickets, for which they paid as "became the blood of the Percies."

"Many scenes in this play," says Davies, Garrick's biographer, "prognosticate to our stage a rising genius in tragedy, who in time will produce scenes not inferior to the best of Otway and Southem, without that mixture of licentiousness and vulgarity which disgrace the productions of these writers."

The success of Percy increased the interest already felt in Hannah More by her London friends. She was beset with engagements and visitations. One day we find her at Sir Joshua's, another at Mrs. Montagu's, with Mrs. Chapone, Mrs. Boscawen, and Miss Carter; another at the Garricks', with the "Sour-crout party," a meeting of learned men once a week at dinner, at which sour-crout always made a dish, and to which Miss More was always invited when she was in town.

"They are playing Percy," writes its author to her sisters, "at this very moment, for the seventh time. I never think of going: it is very odd, but it does not amuse me."

"Last night was the ninth of Percy: it

was a brilliant house, and *I* was there. Lady North did me the honor to take a stage-box. I trembled when the wickedness of going to war was spoken, as I was afraid my Lord was in the house, and that speech, though not written with any particular design, is so bold, and is so warmly received, that it frightens me. Mrs. Montagu had a box again, which, as she is a consummate critic, and is hardly ever seen at a public place, is a great credit to the play. We spent an agreeable evening together at Dr. Cadogan's, where she and I, being the only two monsters in the creation who never touch a card—and laughed at enough we are for it—had the fireside to ourselves, and a more elegant and instructive conversation I have seldom enjoyed. I met Mrs. Chapone one day at Mrs. Montagu's: she is one of Percy's warmest admirers; and as she does not go to plays, but has formed her opinion in the closet, it is more flattering."

"Mrs. Garrick came to me this morning, and wished me to go to the Adelphi, which I declined doing, being so ill. She would have gone herself to fetch me a physician, and insisted upon sending me my dinner, which I refused; but at six this evening, when Garrick came to the Turk's Head to dine, there accompanied him in the coach a minced chicken in the stew-pan, hot, a canister of her fine tea, and a pot of cream. Were there ever such people? Tell it not in epic or lyric that the great Roscius rode with a stew-pan of minced meat with him in the coach, for my dinner. Percy is acted again this evening; do any of you choose to go? For my own part, I shall enjoy a much superior pleasure—that of sitting by the fire, in a good chair, and being denied to all company: what is Percy to this?"

Miss More remained at London during the winter, and in April, 1778, returned to Bristol, where she spent the summer in the quiet enjoyment of home.

CHAPTER V.

DEATH OF GARRICK—THEATRICAL AMUSEMENTS.

THE New-year's greetings of 1779 had scarcely died away before the tidings of Garrick's death startled the English public. Amid the Christmas festivities of Althorp he was suddenly attacked by his old complaint the stone, whose premonitory warnings he had disregarded in leaving home and mingling at all in the gayeties of the season.

Recovering a little, he was carried to London, where it was thought skill and attention might again restore him. The distemper not yielding to the usual remedies, some of the most able practitioners of the city came unbidden to his bedside; but the power of human science and the faithful nursing of his wife availed not. Life was ebbing. His family physician informed him that if he had any worldly affairs to settle, it would be prudent to despatch them as soon as possible.

"I have nothing of that kind to do," answered Garrick, on whose now wan and sunken face the shadow of death was already passing.

Wednesday morning, January 20th, 1779, witnessed his closing act in the great drama of life.

Obedient to the summons of the afflicted wife, Hannah arose from her sick-bed and hastened to the house of death. Mrs. Garrick sunk into her arms. "I have this moment embraced his coffin, and you come next," she exclaimed with a bursting heart; "the goodness of God to me is inexpressible. I do not deserve it, but I am thankful for it."

What a change in the princely mansion! the wit, the genius, the presence of its "well-graced master" were no longer there. Sorrow sat upon every household face, and the rooms were hung with the drapery of mourning.

After mingling her tears and ministering her consolations to the living, she paid a melancholy visit to all that was left of the departed.

"His new house," she says, "is not so pleasant as Hampton or so splendid as the Adelphi, but it is commodious enough for the wants of its inhabitant; and besides, it is so quiet that he will never be disturbed until the eternal morning. May he then find mercy."

The funeral solemnities took place on the first of February, with all the pomp and circumstance of an English public burial, when his body was laid in the poet's corner, beneath the tomb of Shakspeare in Westminster Abbey.

Hannah, accompanied by Miss Cadogan, sat in a little gallery directly over the grave, where she could distinctly hear and see the solemn ceremony. "And this is all of Garrick," was the sad utterance of her heart; "yet a very little while and he shall say to the worm, Thou art my brother; and to corruption, Thou art my mother and my sister. So passes away the fashion of this world."

Miss More, after Garrick's death, wrote two more dramas, "The Fatal Falsehood," and "The Inflexible Captive;" and with these closed her contributions to the stage. This period of intellectual excitement and literary success was brief as it was brilliant; her views of theatrical amusements began to change, and a few years later she came to regard them as dangerous to morals and hostile to Christian virtue.

There are few perhaps whose opinions upon

this subject are more entitled to respect. Her social connections and friendly intercourse with Garrick would have tempted her to view them in the most favorable light, nor could she be accused of any secret or early bias against them, it being then thought no disparagement to the religious character of dignitaries and members of the church to frequent the theatre.

"Why," let us ask, "why write for the stage at all?"

"Because," she replies, "I was led to entertain what I must now think a delusive hope, that the stage, under certain regulations, might be converted into a school of virtue; that though a bad play would always be a bad thing, yet the representation of a good one might become not only harmless, but useful. On these grounds I attempted some theatrical compositions, which, whatever other defects might be justly imputed to them, should at least have been written on the side of virtue and modesty, and which should neither hold out any corrupt image to the mind nor any impure description to the fancy."

Are not then good plays harmless, nay, improving?

"There will still remain," she replies, "even

in tragedies otherwise the most unexceptionable, provided they are sufficiently impassioned to produce a powerful effect on the feelings, and have spirit enough to deserve to become popular, an essential, radical defect. What I insist on is, that there almost inevitably runs through the whole web of the tragic drama a prominent thread of false principle. It is generally the leading object of the poet to erect a standard of *honor*, in direct opposition to the standard of Christianity. Worldly honor is the very soul and spirit and life-giving principle of the drama. It is her moral and political law. Fear and shame are the capital crimes in her code. Love, jealousy, hatred, ambition, pride, revenge, are too often elevated into the rank of splendid virtues, and form a dazzling system of worldly morality in direct contradiction to the spirit of Christianity. The fruits of the Spirit and the fruits of the stage, if the parallel were followed up, would exhibit as pointed a contrast as human imagination could conceive."

What, must the merits of every play be tried by the Ten Commandments?

"We may at least venture to answer, that they should contain nothing *hostile* to them.

If harmless merriment be not expected to *advance* our moral improvement, we must take care that it do not oppose it; for if we concede that our amusements are not expected to make us better than we are, ought we not to be careful that they do not make us worse than they find us? Whatever pleasantry of idea or gayety of sentiment we admit, should we not jealously watch against any unsoundness in the general principle or mischief in the prevailing tendency?"

But what essential difference is there between *reading* a play and *seeing* it acted? Surely one would not object to reading dramatic composition.

"I think there is a substantial difference," she still argues, "between seeing and reading a dramatic composition, and that the objections which lie so strongly against the one, are not, at least in the same degree, applicable to the other. While there is an essential and inseparable danger attendant on dramatic exhibitions, the danger in *reading* a play arises solely from the improper *sentiments* contained in it. It is the semblance of real action which is given to the piece by different persons supporting the different parts, and by their dress, tones, and gestures, heightening the representation into a kind of enchantment. It is the pageantry, the splendor of the spectacle, and even the show of the spectators, these are the circumstances which fill the theatre, produce the effect, and create the danger. These give a pernicious force to sentiments which, when read, may merely explain the mysterious action of the human heart, but which when thus uttered and accompanied, become contagious and destructive. These, in short, make up a scene of temptation and seduction, of overwrought voluptuousness and unnerving pleasure, which ill accords with a desire to be enlightened by the doctrines, or governed by the principles of the gospel of Jesus Christ."

But may not the stage become purified, so as to render it at least harmless and unobjectionable?

"What the stage might be under another and an imaginary state of things, it is not very easy for us to know, and therefore not very important to inquire. Nor is it the soundest logic to argue on the possible goodness of a thing which, in the present circumstances of society, is doing positive evil, from the imagined good that thing might be conjectured to produce in a supposed state of unattainable improvement; for unfortunately nothing can be done until not only the stage itself has undergone complete purification, but until the audience shall be purified also. We must first suppose a state of society in which the spectators will be disposed to relish all that is pure, and to reprobate all that is corrupt, before the system of a pure and uncorrupt theatre can be adopted with any reasonable hope of success: there must always be a harmony between the taste of the spectator and the nature of the spectacle, in order to produce pleasure; for people go to a play not to be instructed, but to be amused."

Let every thoughtful parent, doubting Christian, or tempted youth, read carefully and ponder seriously these positions. There is perhaps no question in Christian education more difficult to settle than what amusements are safe for our children, or what recreations the young Christian, away from the restraints and pastimes of home, may engage in with safety to himself and honor to his divine Master.

We would point the latter to those principles laid down to Wesley by his mother: "Whatever weakens your reason, impairs the tenderness of your conscience, obscures your sense of God, or takes off the relish of spiritual things, in short, whatever increases the strength and authority of your body over your mind, that thing is *sin* to you, however innocent it may be in itself."

And yet you may be placed amid influences which for a time may blind your judgment, and persuade you from your steadfastness: you find yourself overpowered by plausible reasoning, which you cannot readily meet, and because you cannot meet it you are tempted to yield. You are not unlikely to find yourself thus perplexed; what shall you do? Shall you yield without hearty conviction, in deference to the skill or the sneer of your companions?

What shall you do? Refer *to the example of intelligent men and women, eminent for holiness: how have devoted servants of God viewed the subject?* What has been the Christian apprehension of the church upon the matter? It is of no great consequence whether you understand or not the train of thought or course of argument by which their minds were made up and their conduct directed; you have no time, it may be, to examine them if you would: it is enough to know how they acted, and that it will be safe and wise to imitate their example.

Do not hesitate to lean upon an argument like this, in harmony with the spirit of the word of God. It is no sign of weakness to take counsel of the matured judgments of Christian experience, and no sign of manliness to disregard them.

CHAPTER VI.

CORRESPONDENCE.

"HAMPTON, 1780.

"I WISH you a merry Christmas as well as a happy New Year, but that I hate the word merry as so applied; it is a fitter epithet for a bacchanalian than a Christian festival, and seems an apology for idle mirth and injurious excess. What frost, what snow! The vast expanse of glittering white on the ground, the fluid brilliants dropping from the trees, and the green-house full of beautiful blossoms and oranges, make it altogether look like some region of enchantment; and as the gravel walks are all swept clean, I parade an hour or two every morning."

"1781.

"If I commit any sin here or do any good here, it must be in thought, for our words are few and our deeds not at all. Poor Hermes Harris is dead! Everybody is dead, I think; one is almost ashamed of being alive. That you may not think I pass my time quite idly, I must tell you that I had begun Belshazzar;

I like the subject, and have made some progress in it. But that and all my other occupations have given way to the melancholy employment of reading over with Mrs. Garrick all the private letters of the dear deceased master of this melancholy mansion. The employment, though sad, is not without its amusement; it is reading the friendly correspondence of all the men who have made a figure in the annals of business or of literature for the last forty years; for I think I hardly miss a name of eminence in Great Britain, and not many in France: it includes also all his answers, some of the first wits in the country confessing their obligations over and over again to his bounty; money given to some, and lent to such numbers as would be incredible if one did not read it in their own letters. It is not the least instructive part of this employment to consider where almost all these great men are now; the play-writers, where are they? and the poets, are their fires extinguished? Did Lord Bath, or Bishop Warburton, or Lord Chatham, or Goldsmith, or Churchill, or Chesterfield, trouble themselves with thinking that the heads that dictated those bright epistles would so soon be laid low? Did they imagine that such a nobody as I am, whom they would have disdained to have reckoned 'with the dogs of their flock,' should have had the arranging and disposing of them?"

"LONDON, April, 1781.

"I was last Monday at a meeting at the Bishop of St. Asaphs, and had the pleasure of a vast deal of snug chat with the bishop, Mr. Walpole, Mrs. Montagu, and Mrs. Carter.

"Mrs. Kennicott tells me Bishop Lowth insists upon my publishing 'Sensibility,' and all my other poems together, immediately, that people may have them all together. The Dean of Gloucester has sent me his book against Locke, splendidly bound.

"On Friday I dined at Mrs. Boscawen's. We had a snug day and a deal of that social, cordial chat that is so preferable to all the mummery of great parties.

"Tuesday we were a small and choice party at Bishop Shipley's. Lord and Lady Spencer, Lord and Lady Althorpe, Sir Joshua, Boswell, Gibbon, and to my agreeable surprise, Dr. Johnson.

"Mrs. Garrick and he had never met since her bereavement. Johnson came to see us the next morning, and made us a long visit. On

Mrs: Garrick's telling him she was always more at ease with persons who had suffered the same loss with herself, he said that was a comfort she could seldom have, considering the superiority of his merit and the cordiality of their union. He bore his strong testimony of the liberality of Garrick. He reproved me with pretended sharpness for reading Pascal or any of the Port Royal authors, alleging, that as a good Protestant, I ought to abstain from books written by Catholics. I was beginning to stand upon my defence, when he took me with both hands, and with a tear running down his cheeks, 'Child,' said he, with the most affecting earnestness, 'I am heartily glad that you read pious books, by whomsoever they may be written.' "

"On Monday we had a farewell party at Mrs. Vesey's, where we were a little sad to think how many of us might never meet again, particularly poor Mrs. Vesey herself, who is going to Ireland at an advanced age, and in bad health."

"On Tuesday Mrs. Boscawen carried me to Glanvilla; we had the pleasantest tête-à-tête day imaginable, and walked about and sat under the spreading oak, and ate our cold chicken, and drank our tea, as happy folks are wont to do."

In June Miss More returned to her sisters, taking Mrs. Garrick with her, who remained a month at Bristol. Hannah stayed until December, when she again took up her abode in her friend's family.

"Sensibility," a short poem, which a good critic of our own day declares "should be printed in letters of gold," had been passed around in manuscript among her friends, at whose repeated and urgent request it was now published, in company with four sacred dramas.

"The word *sacred* in the title is a damper in the Dramas," writes Miss More. "It is tying a millstone about the neck of 'Sensibility,' which will drown them both together."

"Bishop Lowth has just finished the Dramas, and sent me word, that although I have paid him the most swinging compliment he ever received, he likes the whole book more than he can say. But the Bishop of Chester's compliment is more solid ; he said he thought it would do a vast deal of *good*—and that is the praise best worth having."

"Mrs. Montagu, Chapone, and Carter, are mightily pleased that I have attacked that mock feeling and sensibility which is at once the boast and disgrace of these times, and which is equally deficient in taste and truth. Ask Dr. Stonehouse if he has read 'Cardiphonia,' by Mr. Newton of Olney. There is in it much vital religion, and much of the experience of a good Christian, who feels and laments his own imperfections and weaknesses. I have just finished six volumes of Jortin's sermons; elegant, but cold and very low in doctrine: 'plays round the head, but comes not to the heart;' Cardiphonia does: I like it much, though not every sentiment or expression that it contains."

"On Monday I was at a very great assembly at the Bishop of St. Asaph's. Conceive to yourself one hundred and fifty to two hundred people met together, dressed in the extremity of fashion; painted as red as bacchanals; poisoning the air with perfumes; treading on each other's gowns; making the crowd they blame; not one in ten able to get a chair; protesting they are engaged to ten other places, and lamenting the fatigue they are not obliged to endure; ten or a dozen card-tables crammed with dowagers of quality, grave ecclesiastics, and yellow admirals, and you have an idea of an assembly. I never go to such things when I can possibly avoid it, and stay when there as few minutes as I can."

"London, 1782.

"Poor Johnson is in quite a bad state of health: I fear his constitution is broken up; I am quite grieved at it; he will not leave an abler defender of religion and virtue behind him, and the following little touch of tenderness which I heard of him last night from one of the Turk's Head Club, endears him to me exceedingly. There are always a great many candidates ready, when any vacancy happens in that club, and it requires no small interest and reputation to get elected; but upon Garrick's death, when numberless applications were made to succeed him, Johnson was deaf to them all; he insisted there should be a year's widowhood in the club before they thought of any new election. In Dr. Johnson some contrarieties harmoniously meet; if he has too little charity for the opinions of others, and too little patience with their faults, he has the greatest tenderness for their persons. He told me the other day he hated to hear people whine about metaphysical distresses, when there were so much want and hunger in the world."

"Mrs. Carter and I met at a little breakfast party with a French lady who writes metaphysical books. We got into disgrace by saying that a little common-sense and a little scripture would lead one much farther and safer than volumes of metaphysics. She forgave us, however, on condition we would read two huge quartos which she had just translated. What Mrs. Carter will do I know not, but I shall certainly never fulfil my part of the contract."

In June, Hannah makes a summer flitting to the Kenniçott's at Oxford, where she met Dr. Johnson, and found him sad, sick, and disconsolate.

The death of his friend Mr. Thrale, which had occurred the year before, whose eye for fifteen years, as Johnson tenderly says, "had scarcely been turned upon him but with respect and tenderness," had left a void which nothing filled; "such another friend the general course of human things will not suffer man to hope for." He mournfully adds, "In our walk through life we have dropped our companions, and are now to pick up such as chance may offer to us, or travel alone." As the long shadows of age and ill health crept over him, Dr. Johnson felt the want of those home affections which are our best earthly solace, and which, when the busy interests of early and middle life are over, bear us gently and patiently to our final rest.

In a journey to Oxford at this time, undertaken for the benefit of his health and spirits, the doctor met Miss More, who, grieved at his wan and dejected appearance, made every effort to amuse him. The memory of early days quickened the "old man eloquent," as in her company he retraced the haunts of his college days. On entering a hall, a fine large print of Johnson, handsomely framed, stared upon the party from the opposite wall, with the appended motto, from Miss More's "Sensibility,"

"AND IS NOT JOHNSON OURS, HIMSELF A HOST?"

a pleasing surprise prepared by Dr. Adams, Master of Pembroke, for his distinguished guests.

The doctor remained but a short time; a few beams from the light of early years shot across his path, but they could not renew the joys of youth or lighten the i· firmities of age.

"LONDON, March, 1783.

"On Friday I was at a very fine party at Lady Rothes', where I found a vast many of my friends—Mrs. Montagu, Boscawen, Carter, Thrall, Burney, and Lady Dartry; in short, it was remarked that there was not a woman in London who has been distinguished for taste and literature that was absent. The men were modest and were abashed, the other sex made so strong a party."

"I should be glad to know what our friend Dr. Stonehouse would say to such new-fashioned doctrines as I have lately heard in a charity sermon by a dignified ecclesiastic, and a popular one too, but I will not tell his name: he told the rich and great that they ought to be extremely liberal in their charities, because they were happily *exempted* from the *severer virtues.* How do you like such a sentiment from a Christian teacher? What do you think Polycarp or Ignatius would say to it?"

"March 27.

"I went and sat the other morning with Dr. Johnson, who is far from well. Our conversation was very interesting, but so many came in that I began to feel foolish, and soon sneaked off."

"May 5.

"Saturday we had a dinner at home, Mrs. Carter, Miss Hamilton, the Kennicotts, and Dr. Johnson. Poor Johnson exerted himself exceedingly, but he was very ill, and looked so dreadfully it quite grieved me. His sickness seems to have softened his mind, without at all weakening it. We had but a small party of such of his friends as we knew would be most agreeable to him; and as we were all very attentive, and paid him the homage he both expects and deserves, he was very communicative, and of course instructive and delightful in the highest degree."

"May 22.

"A visitor is just gone, quite chagrined that I am such a rigid Methodist that I cannot come to her assembly on Sunday, though she protests with great piety that she *never has cards*, and that it is quite savage in me to think there can be any harm in a little agreeable music."

While Hannah was at Bristol, during 1784, she became interested for a poor woman in the neighborhood who, in the depths of famine and distress, had exhibited striking poetic talent, and assisted her in preparing a small volume of her poems for the press. The work having been completed, friends were enlisted in its publication.

"I should have taken as much pain as pleasure in the fine stanzas you sent me," responds Mrs. Montagu, "if you had not at the same time assured me you had taken care this noble creature should not want the little comforts of life. I shall most joyfully contribute towards procuring them for her: far, far away all heathen ethics and mythology, geometry and algebra, and make room for the Bible and Milton, when a poet is to be made."

Nearly five hundred pounds were raised upon the book, which were placed in the hands of trustees, and invested in the public funds for the use of the poet and her family. Enraged that the sum was not at her own disposal, the woman turned against her benefactor, and accused her of having embezzled it. So outrageous was her conduct, that no one would hold the trust, and the money fell into her own hands, to be idly squandered, and she died at last destitute and friendless. Of the incident, Hannah says, "I grieve for poor fallen human nature; for as to my own particular part, I am persuaded Providence intends me good by it. Had she turned out well, I should have had my *reward;* as it is, I have my *trial.* Perhaps I was too vain of my success, and in counting over the money might be elated, and think, Is not this great Babylon that *I* have built?"

Two little poems which had been passed around among her friends in manuscript were now published, the Bas Bleu and Florio. Florio was dedicated to Horace Walpole: "It is a paltry return," she writes to him, "for the many hours of agreeable information and elegant amusement which I have received from your spirited and very entertaining writings, and yet I am persuaded you will receive it with favor, as a small offering of esteem and gratitude."

"Poor, dear Johnson," she writes, "is past all hope. I have, however, the comfort to hear that his dread of dying is in a great measure subdued. He sent the other day for Sir Joshua, and after much serious conversation told him he had three favors to beg of him, and he hoped he would not refuse a dying friend, be they what they would. Sir Joshua promised. The first was, that he would never paint on Sunday; the second, that he would give him £30 that he had lent him, as he wanted to leave them to a distressed family; the third, that he would read the Bible whenever he had an opportunity, and that he would never omit it on Sunday."

How solemn are the closing scenes of this dying man. He is styled the Moralist. Justice, truth, virtue, were the pillars of his character; at all times and in all places he was loyal to his convictions of duty, and reverent towards God. In the wide grasp of his clear, calm, comprehensive mind, he everywhere discerned a moral government, and recognized a righteous Governor; his conscience, unseared by passion or self-indulgence, spoke solemnly, and was heard; the fear of God was upon him; but now, as the curtains of death close around his brave heart and unclouded intellect, he lies helpless, wrestling for hope, panting for peace, raising his eyes with a fearful looking for of judgment into the eternal world. "The approach of death is dreadful," he exclaims. "I am afraid to think on that which I know I cannot avoid. It is vain to look round and round for that help which cannot be had; yet we hope and hope, and fancy that he who has lived to-day, may live to-morrow. No wise man will be contented to die, if he thinks he is going into a state of punishment. Nay, no wise man will be contented to die, if he thinks he is to fall into annihilation; for however unhappy any man's existence may be, yet he would rather have it than not exist at all. No; there is no rational principle by which a man can die contented, but a trust in the mercy of God through the merits of Jesus Christ."

And yet when one said to him in an hour of gloomy despondency, "You forget the merits of your Redeemer," he replied with deep solemnity, "I do not forget the merits of my Redeemer, but my Redeemer has said, *He will set some on his right hand and some on his left.*"

"What man," he asks with mournful distrust, "can say that his obedience has been such as he could approve of in another, or that his repentance has not been such as to require being repented of?"

"Remember what you have done by your writings in defence of virtue and truth," urged his friends.

"Admitting all you say to be true," answered the dying hero, "how can I tell when *I have done enough?*"

An awful question, who can answer it?

At last he described the kind of clergyman whom he wished to see. Mr. Winstanley was named, and a note was despatched requesting his attendance in the sick man's chamber. Through ill-health and nervous apprehension, the clergyman could reply only in writing. "Permit me, therefore," ran the note, "to write what I should wish to say, were I present. I can easily conceive what would be the subjects of your inquiry. I can conceive that the views of yourself have changed with your condition, and that on the near approach of death, what you considered mere peccadilloes, have risen into mountains of guilt, while your best actions have dwindled into nothing. On which ever side you look, you see only positive transgression, or defective obedience; and hence, in self-despair, are eagerly asking, 'What shall I do to be saved?' I say to you in the language of the Baptist, 'Behold the Lamb of God.'"

"Does he say so?" exclaimed the anxious listener. "Read it again, Sir John." Upon the second reading, Dr. Johnson declared, "I must see that man, write again to him."

A second letter was the reply, enlarging

upon and enforcing the subject of the first. "These, together with the conversation of a pious friend, Mr. Latrobe, appear to have been blessed of God," continues one in a letter to Hannah More, "in bringing this great man to a renunciation of self, and a simple reliance on Jesus as his Saviour; thus also communicating to him that peace which he had found the world could not give, and which, when the world was fading from his view, was to fill the void, and dissipate the gloom even of the valley of the shadow of death. The man whose intellectual powers had awed all around him, was in turn made to tremble when the period arrived when all knowledge is useless and vanishes away, except the knowledge of the true God and of Jesus Christ whom he has sent. To attain this knowledge, this giant in knowledge must become a little child. The man looked up to as a prodigy of wisdom, must become a fool, that he might be wise."

"For some time before his death all his fears were calmed and absorbed by the prevalence of his faith and his trust in the merit and propitiation of Jesus Christ," testifies Dr. Brocklesby.

"My dear doctor, believe a dying man,"

exclaimed Johnson, "*there is no salvation but in the Lamb of God.*"

"How delighted should I be," said Hannah More, "to hear the dying discourse of this great and good man, especially now that faith has subdued his fears."

CHAPTER VII.

COWSLIP GREEN.

Hitherto Miss More has dwelt in the hearts and by the hearths of beloved friends: sometimes we find her at Sandleford Priory, the country retreat of Mrs. Montagu; her winters were chiefly passed between the Adelphi and Hampton; sometimes she is brushing the dust from the blue stockings at a splendid dinner at Strafford Place, or at a quiet evening at Berkeley-square; lastly, she is nestling with the sisterhood at Bristol. This desultory life was neither aimless nor unimproved; though Miss More had now nearly reached her fortieth year, and as yet had produced little but a few poems, whose chief attractions were their local and personal interest, she had not looked idly on the diversified scenes of men and manners passing around her; from these ample opportunities of understanding the moral defects of English society, she was gathering those materials which enabled her afterwards to speak so powerfully and successfully in the parlors and palaces of England.

The death of Garrick deeply impressed her. It made an abrupt and solemn pause in her social and intellectual enjoyments. His taste and genius, his sympathy and interest, delighted and dazzled her. Her literary tastes were banqueted; the amplest opportunities to enlarge and cultivate her powers were placed at her disposal; and more than all, she was encouraged to enter that field of literature towards which she seems to have had a strong and early bias: nay, she had entered the lists, and "Percy" had been crowned with laurels.

Garrick died; it was the first death in the gay circle which had first welcomed her to London, and it left a void never to be filled. In the long shadow which it cast over his home, Hannah sat and thought. She saw the fashion of the world with its pomps and praises passing away. Could these satisfy the hunger of the soul? What was that greater good, worthy the energies of her whole being? She felt deep within her that it was not *all* of life to live, nor *all* of death to die: a conviction that life had a wider sphere, nobler motives, higher aims, and more exalted hopes, than literary ambition or intellectual enjoyments could give fastened itself upon her. She saw *ac-*

countability to God, written as with a pen of fire upon her time and talents. In the devout solitude of her closet, her solemnized spirit holds communion with eternal realities; all earthly things seem paltry and worthless, compared with the favor of God: she inquires with serious earnestness what is essential to duty and acceptance in Jesus Christ? what are the laws of holy living prescribed in his gospel? how can the authority of conscience be maintained amid the conflicts of passion, of sense, and of worldly engagements? how run the Christian race; how win the heavenly prize? The higher life of the soul began to dawn upon her.

"I have naturally a small appetite for grandeur," she says, "which is always satisfied, even to indigestion, before I leave town, and I require a long abstinence to get any relish for it again. Yet I repeat, there are very agreeable people; but there is dress, there is restraint, there is want of leisure, to which I find it more difficult to conform for any length of time—and *life is short*."

One thing which greatly aided her in maintaining an habitual thoughtfulness of mind amid the giddy disregard of sacred things in much of the society in which she mixed, was her *strict observance of holy time.* The Sabbath was always to her a day of rest—rest from society, from visiting, from all worldly occupations and engagements: she used it as it was designed to be used by its great Author—as a day of religious improvement, a means of holy living, sacred to God and eternal things. Wherever she was, in whatever company she happened to be, she was never afraid of appearing singular, by a devout and respectful observance of the Lord's day.

"You know I often told you," she wrote home while a resident at the Adelphi, "that Sunday is not only my day of rest, but enjoyment; I go twice to the churches where I expect the best preaching, frequently at St. Clements, to hear my excellent friend Burrows. Mrs. Garrick declines asking company on Sunday on my account, so that I enjoy the whole day to myself. After my more select reading, I attack South, Atterbury, and Warburton. In these great geniuses and original thinkers, I see many passages of Scripture presented in a strong and striking light. I think it right to mix their learned labors with the devout effusions of more spiritual writers,

Baxter, Doddridge, Hopkins, Jeremy Taylor—the Shakspeare of divinity—and the profound Barrow in turn. I devour much, but I fear digest little. In the evening I read a sermon and prayers to the family, which Mrs. Garrick likes much."

Miss More had for some time gradually contracted her circle of acquaintance, confining her visits to smaller assemblies and choicer friends.

"I have kept my resolution," she says, "to avoid great crowds, except when I have been snared into one under the alluring name of a little private party, into which trap I have fallen several times. On Saturday I got a sober day at Mrs. Montagu's, with only the Smelts, and we all agreed we had not been more comfortable for a long time; and yet people rarely have the sense or courage to do these things, but must still meet in herds and flocks."

She now began to yearn for a home of her own, where she could enjoy undisturbed retirement, hedged in from the great world, to pursue her course of thought, of reading, and of occupation, more in harmony with the natural simplicity of her tastes, and the progressive development of her religious character. When her purpose of doing so became known, the notion was assailed with ridicule and argument, and not a few agreed in predicting her speedy and permanent return to London and Bristol.

In spite of forebodings and dissuasives, Miss More at length fixed upon a small establishment in the parish of Wrington, ten miles from Bristol, so secluded from the hum of the great world as to be unvisited even by the post. It was a thatched-roof cottage; flowers edge the walks and fringe the green lawn, which slopes gently towards the south, diversified by groups of shrubbery pleasing to the eye, and affording a refreshing shade from the noontide heats. Beyond in the dusky distance rises the Mendip Ridge, bold and grand. Behold Cowslip Green; Horace Walpole called it a country cousin to Strawberry-hill.

"I am fitting up a tiny boudoir at Cowslip Green," says the new mistress of the cottage, "which I intend shall contain no literature but the offerings of kindness: by this means my imagination will convert my little closet into a temple of friendship; and when the weather is bad, or my spirits low, what a cordial it will be to fancy that I am loved and esteemed by so many amiable and worthy people as there have contributed to my instruction and delight!"

"What book shall I send?" asks Mr. Pepys, one of her friends and favorites. "To send you a skimming-dish or fish-kettle towards setting up housekeeping would be making too little distinction between you and the next good housewife in the parish; but if you would be so good as to tell me any pleasant companion who is not already of your party, I should have particular pleasure in sending him, and should be very much flattered with the idea that on some lonely evening he might recall me to your memory."

"I am mightily at a loss," she humorously replies, "what book you will send. What think you of a cook-book? No, that wont do either, for it will introduce sauces and luxury, and all manner of cunningly devised dishes and extravagant inventions into a little cottage devoted to simplicity, and from which aspiring thoughts and luxurious desires are to be entirely excluded. I should beg a wooden dish and maple spoon, but that it is pleasanter to one's friends to be remembered in one's more intellectual hours. Pray take notice, it must not be a *fine new book* out of the shop; that would destroy the charm, which lies in this, that the book must be transplanted from the library of a friend."

She afterwards wrote to the same gentleman: "After living melodious days with Mrs. Montagu, the nightingales, and Spenser, I have now been quietly set down in my cottage a month, and the evil days have not come wherein you barbarously prophesied that I should feel a joy even to see the apothecary ride up to the door, though it is certain I never *do* see him without thinking of you. I do not express myself very accurately when I talk of living quietly; for, in truth, my neighbors are so kind, and so many people have brought themselves into the description, that I am far from enjoying that perfect retreat which I had figured to myself. I work in my garden all the morning, and ride in the evening through delicious lanes and hills: my most serious studies have been a little book of Mrs. Trimmer's, that wise and pleasant friend of little children; it is a most delectable history of Robin Redbreast."

In relation to the temptations which clogged her spiritual progress in the new home which she had chosen, she thus expresses herself to Rev. John Newton:

"The care of my garden gives me employment, health, and spirits. I want to know, dear sir, if it is peculiar to myself to form ideal plans of perfect virtue, and to dream of all manner of imaginary goodness in untried circumstances, while one neglects the immediate duties of one's actual situation? Do I make myself understood? I have always fancied that if I could secure to myself such a quiet retreat as I have now really accomplished, I should be wonderfully good; that I should have leisure to store my mind with such and such maxims of wisdom; that I should be safe from such and such temptations; that, in short, my whole summers would be smooth periods of peace and goodness. Now the misfortune is, I have actually found a great deal of the comfort I expected, but without any of the concomitant virtues. I am certainly happier here than in the agitation of the world, but I do not find that I am one bit better; with full *leisure* to rectify my heart and affections, the disposition unluckily does not come. I have the mortification to find that petty and—as they are called—innocent employments can detain my heart from heaven as much as tumultuous pleasures. If to the pure all things are pure, the reverse must be also true, when I can contrive to make so harmless an employment as the cultivation of flowers stand in the room of a vice, by the great portion of time I give up to it, and by the entire dominion it has over my mind. You will tell me that if the affections be estranged from their proper object, it signifies not much whether a bunch of roses or a pack of cards affects it. I pass my life in intending to get the better of this, but life is passing away, and the reform never begins. It is a very significant saying, though a very old one, of one of the Puritans, that 'hell is paved with good intentions!' I sometimes tremble to think how large a square my procrastination alone may furnish to this tesselated pavement."

"What you are pleased to say, my dear madam, of the state of your mind, I understand perfectly well," answers this good man, who well understood the deceitfulness of the human heart; "I praise God on your behalf, and I hope I shall earnestly pray for you. I have stood upon that ground myself.

"We are apt to wonder that, when what we accounted hinderances are removed, and the things which we conceived would be great advantages are put within our power, still there is a secret something in the way, which proves itself to be independent of all external changes, because it is not affected by them. The disorder we complain of is internal; and in allusion to our Lord's words upon another occasion, I may say, it is *not any thing in our outward situation*—provided it be not actually unlawful—that can *prevent or even retard our advances* in religion; we are defiled and impeded by that which is within. So far as our hearts are right, all places and circumstances which this wise and good providence allots us are nearly equal: their hinderances will prove helps, losses gains, and crosses will ripen into comforts; but till we are so far apprized of the nature of our disease as to put ourselves into the hands of the great and only Physician, we shall find, like the woman in Luke 8:43, that every other effort for relief will leave us as it found us.

"Our first thought when we begin to be displeased with ourselves, and sensible that we have been wrong, is to attempt to reform; to be sorry for what is amiss, and to endeavor to amend. It seems reasonable to ask, What can we do more? but while we think we can do so much as this, we do not fully understand the design of the gospel. This gracious message from the God who knows our frame speaks home to our case. It treats us as *sinners*—as those who have already broken the original law of our nature in departing from God our Creator, supreme Lawgiver, and Benefactor, and of having lived to ourselves instead of devoting all our time, talents, and influence to his glory. As *sinners*, the first things we need are pardon, reconciliation, and a principle of life and conduct entirely new.

"For these purposes we are directed to Jesus Christ, as the wounded Israelites were to look at the brazen serpent. John 3:14, 15. When we understand what the Scripture teaches of the person, love, and offices of Christ, the necessity and final cause of his humiliation unto death, and feel our own need of such a Saviour, we then know him to be the light, the sun of the world and of the soul; the source of all spiritual light, life, comfort, and influence; having access by God to him, and receiving out of his fulness grace for grace.

"Our perceptions of these things are for a time faint and indistinct, like the peep of dawn; but the dawning light, though faint, is the sure harbinger of approaching day.

"The beginnings of spiritual life are small in the true Christian; *he* passes through a succession of various dispensations, but he advances, though silently and slowly, yet surely, and will stand for ever.

"At the same time, it must be admitted that the Christian life is a warfare. Much within us and much without us must be resisted. In such a world as this, and with such a nature as *ours*, there will be a call for habitual self-denial. We must learn to cease from depending upon our own supposed wisdom, power, and goodness, and from self-complacency and self-seeking, that we may rely upon Him whose wisdom and power are infinite."

What individual, earnestly striving for a better life, has not sighed over the clogs and hinderances which beset his path, and which he fondly imagines other situations are exempt from? Were this wish fulfilled, were that place attained, another goal reached, this obstacle removed, then how easy the yoke, how light the burden, how smooth the way! Alas, no situation is free from straits and perplexities; nowhere are we exempt from the necessity of watchfulness and combat. The evil is within us. "The things that we would, we do not; and the things that we would not, those we do." "The flesh lusteth against the spirit, and the spirit against the flesh, and these are contrary the one to the other." In this perpetual conflict how can the victory be secured? Only by watchfulness and prayer through our Lord Jesus Christ.

CHAPTER VIII.

FIRST FRUITS.

From the time Cowslip Green was made her home in 1785, may be dated higher views of duty, a more confirmed religious character, and a clearer comprehension of her sphere of usefulness. As the retreat was not sought for day-dreaming leisure, her time was not whiled away in literary effeminacy, nor her pen given to pleasing fictions. Hannah More soon found she had a work to do for the day and generation in which she lived, and vigorously she wrought it out.

The first fruit of Cowslip Green was a small book, entitled, "Thoughts on the Importance of the Manners of the Great to General Society," an introductory chapter to that elevated series of Christian teaching which became the business of her life.

It first appeared anonymously, "not so much for the fear of man," she says, "which worketh a snare, as because, if anonymous, it may be ascribed to some better person, and because I fear I do not live as I write. I hope it may be useful to myself at least, as I give a sort of public pledge of my principles, to which I pray I may be enabled to act up."

It was at first attributed to Wilberforce, then to the Bishop of London. Its author yet unknown, the book being canvassed in her presence, she was abruptly asked if she could conjecture who wrote it. "Whoever the author may be, I doubt not the writer was in earnest," replied Miss More with the utmost self-possession. But it did not long remain a secret. She received at last an anonymous epigram.

"Of sense and religion in this little book,
All agree there's a wonderful store;
But while round the world for an author they look,
I only am wishing for *More*."

This was her first attack upon the ungodly habits and minor immoralities of the age: her long and intimate acquaintance with the higher ranks of English society, for whom, as the title indicates, the book was expressly written, enabled her to write with truth and directness: she knew whereof she spoke. "Yet I have not gone deep," she says; "it is confined to prevailing practical evils: should this succeed, I hope by the blessing of God to attack the principle." Rev. John Newton congratulates her upon the choice of a subject, and a subject too most admirably handled. She skilfully describes the features and influence of that large class, abounding in every community, called *good sort of people*—people who live within the restraints of moral obligation, and acknowledge the truth of the Christian religion, yet whose views terminate with this world's good, and who are destitute of that first essential principle of human actions, which can alone render them of any value in the sight of God, faith in Christ. It is not so much what they do, as what they *neglect* to do, which constitutes at once the danger to themselves and others; it is the *coming short* which is so full of peril. Alas, how many such are there all around, pleasant neighbors, generous friends, worthy citizens, whose prudence, kindness, integrity, honored and respected by the world, constitute no claim to acceptance before that tribunal which, searching the heart, declares, "Without holiness no man shall see the Lord."

The habit of employing hair-dressers upon the Sabbath, of giving "card money" to servants, and requiring them to dismiss a visitor with a "Not at home," Sunday concerts, and Sunday diversions were each in turn commented upon and condemned, in a spirit at once so kind, so candid, so decided, that the book commended itself alike to reason and consistency, and challenged an impartial reading even from those most amenable to its reproofs.

On her next meeting Horace Walpole, he took her to task for having exhibited such monstrously severe doctrines. "He defended, and that was the joke," writes she to her sisters, "religion against me, and said he would do so against the whole bench of bishops—that the fourth commandment was the most amiable and merciful law that was ever promulgated, as it entirely considers the ease and comfort of the hard-laboring poor and beasts of burden; but that it was never intended for persons of fashion, who have no occasion for rest, as they never do any thing on the other days; and indeed, when the law was made there were no people of fashion. He really pretended to be in earnest, and we parted mutually unconverted; he lamenting I had fallen into the error of *puritanical* strictness, and I lamenting he is a person of fashion, for whom the ten commandments are not made!"

The book made its way: when the second edition was issued it sold in little more than a week; the third in a few hours; and seven large editions disappeared in a few months: extensively read and circulated, it did not fail to exercise a vast influence in the circles for whom it was chiefly intended; its admonitions were heard and heeded; several of these customs fell into disrepute, and at last were entirely abandoned. For these beneficial changes society is indebted to Miss Hannah More.

Two years afterwards an "Estimate of the Religion of the Fashionable World" appeared, striking deep at the false principles which govern men in their daily lives, and laying bare the inconsistencies and hollow professions of those who bore the Christian name.

The estimate is full of sound, clear, and discriminating views, applicable quite as much to our time as it was to the spirit and tendencies of eighty years ago.

"The present age," she says, "may justly be called the age of benevolence. Liberality flows with a full tide through a thousand channels. There is scarcely a newspaper that does not record some meeting of men of fortune for the most salutary purposes. The noble and numberless structures for the relief of distress, which are the ornament and glory of our metropolis, proclaim species of munificence unknown to former ages. Subscriptions are easily solicited.

"Allowing the boasted superiority of modern benevolence, it might be well to inquire whether the diffusion of this branch of charity, though the most lovely offspring of religion, be yet any positive proof of the prevalence of religious principle; and whether it be not the fashion rather to consider benevolence as a substitute for Christianity than as an evidence of it?"

Are not these questions pertinent also to us in our day?

"It seems to be one of the reigning errors among some," she continues, "to reduce all religion into benevolence, and all benevolence into alms-giving. The wide and comprehensive idea of Christian charity is compressed into the slender compass of a little pecuniary relief. This species of benevolence is indeed a bright gem among the ornaments of a Christian, but by no means furnishes all the jewels of a crown which derives its lustre from the associated radiance of every Christian grace.

"The mere casual benevolence of any man can have little claim to solid esteem; nor does any charity deserve the name which does not grow out of a steady conviction that it is his bounden duty; which does not spring from a settled propensity to obey the whole will of God; which is not therefore made a part of the general plan of his conduct; and which does not lead him to order the whole scheme of his affairs with an eye to it.

"He therefore who does not habituate himself to certain interior restraints, who does not live in a regular course of self-renunciation, will not be likely often to perform acts of beneficence, when it becomes necessary to convert to such purposes any of that time or money which appetite, temptation, or vanity solicit him to divert to other purposes.

"And surely he who seldom sacrifices one darling indulgence, who does not subtract one gratification from the incessant round of his enjoyments, when the indulgence would obstruct his capacity of doing good, or when the sacrifice would enlarge his power, does not deserve the name of *benevolent*. And for such an unequivocal criterion of charity, to whom are we to look but to the conscientious Christian? No other spirit but that by which he is governed can subdue self-love; and where self-love is the predominant passion, benevolence can have but a feeble or an accidental dominion.

"Now if we look around and remark the excesses of luxury, the costly diversions, and the intemperate dissipation in which numbers of professing Christians indulge, can any stretch of candor, can even that tender sentiment by which we are enjoined 'to hope' and to 'believe all things,' enable us to hope and believe that such are actuated by a spirit of Christian benevolence, merely because we see them perform some casual acts of charity, which the spirit of the world can contrive to make extremely compatible with a voluptuous life, and the cost of which, after all, bears but little proportion to that of any one vice, or even vanity?"

The whole treatise is worth a thorough reading, abounding as it does with good sense and sound piety. The Bishop of London declared there were few persons in Great Britain who could write a book conveying so much evangelical morality, and so much genuine Christianity, in such neat and elegant language, and predicted that the book would find its way into every fine lady's library, and if not into her heart and manners, the fault would be her own.

A letter from Mrs. Chapone thus expresses her commendation:

"The same good gentleman, my dear madam, who some time ago gave his excellent thoughts to 'the Great,' has again made a powerful effort for their reformation, which they receive with as much avidity as if they meant to be amended by it: indeed, he has wisely recommended it to their taste by every charm and ornament of eloquence.

"He has been so obliging as to send me a copy of his admirable book, and as I do not know his name and address, I take the liberty of applying to you—who are, I believe, pretty well acquainted with him, though probably not aware of half his merits—to beg you will convey to him my grateful acknowledgments for his favor, and assure him that he continually rises in my esteem by the faithful zeal with which he lays out the talents intrusted to him at the highest interest; and I will venture to confess, gentleman though he be, that I sincerely love and honor him, and wish the most perfect success to all his laudable undertakings.

"We long for you in town, my dear Miss More; hasten and enjoy the applause your lay friend has gained, and to which his own heart must bear testimony."

Two choice spirits had been added to her list of friends, Rev. John Newton and William Wilberforce, both of whom quickened her in the new and honorable career opening before her.

Of Wilberforce and the great subject that first linked them together, she thus writes to Mrs. Carter:

"This most important cause, the project to abolish the slave-trade in Africa, has very much occupied my thoughts this summer; the young gentleman, Mr. Wilberforce, who has embarked in it with the zeal of an apostle, has been much with me, and engaged all my little interest and all my affections in it. It is to be brought before Parliament in the spring. Above one hundred members have promised their votes. My dear friend, be sure to canvass everybody who has a heart. It is a subject too ample for a letter, and I shall have a great deal to say to you on it when we meet. To my feelings, it is the most interesting subject which was ever discussed in the annals of humanity."

At twenty-six Wilberforce was a member of Parliament, master of an ample fortune, surrounded by friends and flatterers, treading a path sown with temptations, pleasures, and vices, all tending to corrupt the morals and mislead the judgment. On a continental tour to recruit during a recess of Parliament, in company with a friend, a little book became the companion of their journey—a little book which asked no favors, uttered no flatteries, and could expect little countenance from one like Wilberforce. "It is one of the best little books ever written though," said his friend, who respected its bravery and truth. "Let us read it then," replied Wilberforce; and so the two journeyed and read. "I will search the Scriptures and see if these things are so," said Wilberforce, as he read and was astonished. The book was Doddridge's Rise and Progress of Religion in the Soul, whose appeals and persuasions, whose rebukes and denunciations the young man found recorded and reiterated on every page of the Bible. Wilberforce saw his danger, and fled for refuge to the cross of Christ.

Immediately on his return to England he sought the spiritual guidance of John Newton. Wilberforce soon appeared a changed man. In his consecration to the service of his divine Master, there was no reserve or compromise; he gave up himself and his all: "Henceforth let me do with my might while the day lasts," was the sleepless endeavor of his life.

A society for the reformation of public morals was soon set on foot through his instrumentality, which helped greatly to check the spread of blasphemous and indecent publications, and was the source of many kindred schemes for the public good.

But the abolition of the slave-trade was the great work which must immortalize Wilberforce, and at twenty-eight, 1787, he allied himself to its interests. While making a short sojourn at Bath for the benefit of its waters, during the autumn of this year, he records of himself, "I believe one cause of my having fallen so short, is my having aimed no higher. Remember, thy situation abounding in comforts requires thee to be peculiarly on thy guard, lest when thou hast eaten and art full, thou forgettest God;" yet Miss More, who now passed much time in his society, declares, "This young gentleman's character is one of the most extraordinary I ever knew for talents, virtue, and piety. It is difficult not to grow wiser and better every time one converses with him."

The enormities of the slave traffic had long attracted the attention of thoughtful and feeling minds, both in England and America. Seven years before, Mr. Burke had nearly determined to bring the subject before the English Parliament, having sketched a bill to provide for the immediate amelioration of its severities as well as for its ultimate extinction; the measure, however, he abandoned, from a conviction that it would prove unpopular and ruinous to his party.

Meanwhile much was done to arouse and inform the public mind. In May, 1787, several gentlemen met together in London, and formed themselves into a committee to collect information and raise funds for promoting the abolition of the trade. Over this body Granville Sharpe presided, while Clarkson, with his untiring zeal, was kindling the public conscience against it.

And now the subject is to be laid before Parliament—where is the man of moral mettle to undertake it? No man of party connection or political ambition dared engage in a work of such doubtful and dangerous issues. It must be undertaken at his own peril, depending alone on the righteousness of his cause, for commercial power and self-interest, wealth and long usage were all too ready to defend it. Wilberforce was the man. How bravely he battled, and how glorious the issue, the world knows well.

Among the publications of the day to arouse and enlist the public sympathies, "The Slave-trade," a little poem, came from the pen of Hannah More.

CHAPTER IX.

LABORS AMONG THE POOR—SUNDAY-SCHOOLS.

On New-year's day of 1789, Miss More is dining at Berkeley-square, Mrs. Montagu having assembled around her a few of the Blues, among whom we recognize the familiar face of Mrs. Boscawen.

Mrs. Vesey was in that state of illness which left nothing to hope—her mind was gone.

"Ah," sighed Miss More on visiting her, "it is melancholy to look at this house, where I have seen so many agreeable people, and heard so much pleasant conversation, and made so many friendships, and think that its mistress is bereft of her faculties. What a call for serious reflection! I want to get my heart more affected with feeling for the sorrows of others, and with gratitude for my own mercies."

She soon after went down to Hampton, where she passed a few weeks each year to cheer the widowed heart of Mrs. Garrick.

The exciting topic of the spring was the slave question, about to be laid before Parliament. Wilberforce went to Teston to consult his advisers and marshal his forces for the approaching debate. "He with the whole junto of abolitionists are slaving it till two o'clock every morning," declares Mrs. Bouverie. "I hope Teston will be the Runnymede of the negroes," ejaculates Miss More, "and the great charter of African liberty will be completed: the fate of Africa now trembles in the balance."

On the 12th of May, in a speech of three hours of surpassing eloquence, Wilberforce opened the debate in the House of Commons, denouncing the slave-trade as a national iniquity, and tracing with masterly power its destructive effects upon Africa, upon its victims, and upon the colonies. Viewed from the elevated height of a common humanity and a Christian civilization, he saw its horrors and injustice in all their length, breadth, and depth, and his soul glowed with the magnitude of the subject. Pitt, Burke, and Fox gave him a strong and eloquent support, each unanimously declaring that the slave-trade was a disgrace to the country, and that nothing but its entire abolition could satisfy the demands of justice and humanity. It was a glorious night for England. Principles familiar to us as household words were then broached as dangerous and startling innovations, and were met by a powerful opposition from the callous, the timid, and the self-interested.

Miss More soon left these exciting scenes for a June flitting to Rosedale, Mrs. Boscawen's new villa at Richmond, "and I am sitting," she closes a letter to Martha, "on the very seat where Thomson wrote his Seasons."

Then followed a visit to Sandleford, whose Gothic windows, Grecian wit, and British oaks, could not ward off five days of unrelenting headache, to which Miss More from early life was subject; next a sail down the Wye, in company with Mr. and Miss Wilberforce; next at Stoke, dwelling in sober magnificence with a certain dowager duchess, where "a little more discretion and a little less fancy were proper and decorous," as she tells us.

Hannah and Martha are now at Cowslip Green: the retreat is enlivened by a day from Mrs. Montagu, a week from Mrs. Garrick, both of whom came to try the benefit of Bath waters, and a fortnight from Mrs. Kennicott, "who with wonderful readiness accommodated herself to the quiet, simple life of their little cottage;" then came a vacation week from the elder sisterhood, and last, though not least, the Wilberforces made a ramble to the Green.

Among the interesting features of the surrounding scenery, rose the bold and romantic cliffs of Cheddar, forming a picturesque perspective towards the south ten miles from Cowslip Green. Among these cliffs were scenes of wild beauty and solemn grandeur, yawning caverns, damp hollows, and bald peaks, which made them the summer resort of many a traveller.

The sisters begged Wilberforce not to leave Wrington without a visit to these wonders of the region. Patty was eloquent, and urged the gratification which the drive would give to a mind like his: a day was fixed, then given up; the cliffs were discussed at the breakfast-table the next morning, until their guest was prevailed upon to go.

On his return, Patty ran into the parlor, triumphantly inquiring how he liked the Cliffs.

"Very fine," he replied; "but the poverty and distress of the people are dreadful."

"This was all that passed," said Patty, in

relating the circumstance. "Wilberforce soon retired to his room, and dismissed even his reader. I said to Hannah and his sister that I feared he was not well. The cold chicken and wine put into the carriage for his dinner were returned untouched. Mr. Wilberforce appeared at supper, seemingly refreshed with a higher feast than we had sent with him. The servant at his desire was dismissed, when immediately he began: 'Miss Hannah More, something must be done for Cheddar.'

"He then gave us a particular account of his day, of the inquiries he had made respecting the poor: there was no resident minister, no manufactory, nor did there appear any dawn of comfort, either temporal or spiritual. The possibility and method of assisting them were discussed till a late hour: it was then decided in a few words, by Mr. Wilberforce's exclaiming, 'If you will be at the trouble, I will be at the expense.'

"Something commonly called an impulse crossed my heart, that told me it was God's work, and it would do: and though I never nave, and probably never shall recover the same emotion, yet it is my business to water it with watchfulness.

"Mr. Wilberforce and his sister left us in a day or two. We turned many schemes in our head every possible way; at length those measures were adopted which led to the formation of the different schools."

The Cliffs of Cheddar at this time were inhabited by a squalid, ignorant, half-savage people, dwelling in the caves and fissures of the rocks, and earning a miserable subsistence by selling roots, stalactites, and other mineral productions to the travellers who visited them.

The hearts of the sisters had already yearned over the destitution and wretchedness of this forlorn community, and they readily responded to the call. Home missionary work of this kind was then comparatively new: Robert Raikes had begun to bless Gloucester with the Sunday-school, and two hundred and fifty thousand children were already enjoying its privileges, yet the inestimable benefits of the institution were not yet widely known or fully realized; old Brentford also was reaping a harvest of good from the warm-hearted efforts of good Mrs. Trimmer. These labors had received Hannah More's cordial sympathy and warm approval: a similar field was now open to her, and she instantly determined to occupy it. Accompanied by Patty, she explored the region, a graphic account of which she pens to Wilberforce in a letter dated George Hotel, Cheddar.

"Though this is but a romantic place, as my friend Matthew well observed, yet you would laugh to see the bustle I am in. I was told that we should meet with great opposition if I did not try to propitiate the chief despot of the village, who is very rich and very brutal: so I ventured into the den of this monster, in a country as savage as himself, near Bridgewater. He begged that I would not think of bringing any religion into the country; it was the worst thing in the world for the poor, it made them lazy and useless. In vain I represented to him that they would be more industrious as they were better principled; and that for my own part, I had no selfish views in what I was doing. He gave me to understand that he knew the world too well to believe either the one or the other. Somewhat dismayed to find that my success bore no proportion to my submissions, I was almost discouraged from more visits; but I found that friends must be secured at all events; for if these rich savages set their faces against us, and influenced the poor people, I saw that nothing but hostilities would ensue; so I made eleven more of these agreeable visits; and as I improved in the art of canvassing, had better success. Miss Wilberforce would have been shocked had she seen the petty tyrants whose insolence I stroked and tamed, the ugly children I praised, the pointers and spaniels I caressed, the cider I commended, and the wine I swallowed. After these irresistible flatteries, I inquired of each if he could recommend me to a house; and said that I had a little plan which I hoped would secure their orchards from being robbed, their rabbits from being shot, their game from being stolen, and which might lower the poor-rates. If effect be the best proof of eloquence, then mine was a good speech, for I gained at length the hearty concurrence of the whole people, and their promise to discourage or favor the poor in proportion as they were negligent or attentive in sending their children. Patty, who is with me, says she has good hopes that the hearts of some of these rich poor wretches may be touched: they are as ignorant as the beasts that perish, intoxicated every day before dinner, and plunged into such vices as make me begin to think London a virtuous place. By their assistance I procured immediately a good house, which, when a partition is taken down and a window added, will receive a great number of children. The house and an excellent garden of almost an acre of ground, I have taken at once for six guineas and a half a year. I have ventured to take it for seven years. There is courage for you. It is to be put in order immediately, 'for the night cometh;' and it is a comfort to think that though I may be in dust and ashes in a few weeks, yet by that time this business will be in actual motion. I have written to different manufacturing towns for a mistress, but can get nothing hitherto. As to the mistress for the Sunday-school and the religious part, I have employed Mrs. Esterbrook, of whose judgment I have a good opinion. I hope Miss W—— will not be frightened, but I am afraid she must be called a Methodist.

"I asked the farmers if they had no resident curate. They told me they had a right to insist on one; which right they confessed they had never ventured to exercise, for fear their tithes would be raised. I blushed for my species. The glebe-house is good for my purposes. The curate lives at Wells, twelve miles distant. They have only service once a week, and there is scarcely an instance of a poor person being visited or prayed with."

In spite of Miss Hannah's repeated headaches, and Miss Patty's ill-health, so promptly and energetically did they pursue their labors, that the first of October witnessed the opening of the school in Cheddar, by Miss Hannah in person. The principal people from the parishes far and near came to witness the operation of a scheme, as it was regarded, to reform Botany Bay.

"It was an affecting sight," says she. "Several of the grown up youth had been tried at the late assizes, three were the children of a person lately condemned to be hanged; many thieves, all ignorant, profane, and vicious beyond belief. Of this banditti we have enlisted one hundred and seventy; and when the clergyman, a hard man, who is also the magistrate, saw these creatures kneeling around us, whom he had seen but to commit or to punish in some way, he burst into tears. I can do them but little good, I fear, but the grace of God can.

"Have you never felt your mind," she

asks Wilberforce, "now and then raised and touched by some very trifling circumstance? So I felt on Sunday. Some musical gentleman, drawn from a distance by curiosity—just as I was coming out of church with my ragged regiment, much depressed to think how little good I could do them—quite unexpectedly struck up that beautiful and animated anthem, 'Inasmuch as ye have done it to one of the least of these, ye have done it unto me.'"

To the Sunday-school was soon added a school during the week, where sewing, knitting, and spinning were taught to the girls. A faithful and excellent woman was engaged as mistress of this school, who, with her daughter, entered completely into Miss More's plans; medicine, clothing, and small sums of money were from time to time placed at her disposal to distribute among the sick and needy, according to her judgment.

Two years after Miss More's first visit to Cheddar, she received a zealous ally in the Rev. Thomas Drewitt, who became a resident curate among this people, strengthening her hands, and encouraging her heart by all the means in his power.

Great as was the work for Cheddar, Cheddar did not bound their hopes or exhaust their energies: other fields opened before them, and they went boldly forward bearing the precious seed; thirteen parishes were found equally destitute of the means of social comfort or religious improvement. In Shipham the women knew nothing of industry or frugality, the young men spent the Sabbath in sporting and hunting, and the children grew up in nakedness and vagrancy. At Axbridge the curate was intoxicated six times in the week, and very frequently was prevented from preaching by two black eyes, honestly earned by fighting; the ale-house was more frequented than the church, the laws of cards or quoits were better understood than the ten commandments, while good order and domestic peace were things unheard of.

"The lower classes are *fated* to be poor, ignorant, and wicked," said the petty landholders; "and wise as you are, you cannot alter what is decreed." "Besides," added another, "I like the parish very well as it is; if the young men come and gamble before my house Sunday afternoon, I have only to go out and curse and swear at them, and they will march off; what can one desire more?"

Happily for the parishes, there were those who *did* desire more; there were time and talent and money that had been consecrated to the Lord's service, and were to be spent for their good: before the year closed, schools were established in nine different parishes; and five hundred scholars were enjoying the benefits of Sabbath-day instruction.

From Bath, Wilberforce wrote to Miss More: "I have more money than time, and if you or your sister will condescend to be my almoner, you will enable me to employ some of the superfluity it has pleased God to give me, to some good purpose. Sure am I, that they who subscribe attention and industry furnish articles of more sterling and intrinsic value. Besides, I have a rich banker in London, Mr. Henry Thornton, whom I cannot oblige so much as by drawing on him for purposes like these. I shall take the liberty of enclosing a draft for £40; but this is only for a beginning."

"I joyfully accept your office of almoner," replies Hannah, "on condition that you will find fault with and direct me with as little scruple as I shall have in disposing of your money. Patty is very proud at being admitted into the confederacy, and at being appointed superintendent at Cheddar; a title, however, she will only hold by delegation in my too long absence, for I like my dignity too well to allow her to be more than vice-queen.

"What comfort I feel, in looking round on these starving and half-naked multitudes, to think that by your liberality many of them may be fed and clothed: and Oh, if but one soul is rescued from eternal misery, how may we rejoice over it in another state, where perhaps it may not be one of our smallest felicities that our friendship was turned to some useful account in advancing the good of others, and as I humbly presume to hope, in improving ourselves for that life which shall have no end.

"Mr. Henry Thornton, I think, belongs to the Society of Sunday-schools in London for assisting necessitous villages with books, etc. There cannot be a fairer claim on them than the present. If you and he approve it, perhaps we may apply for a quantity of New Testaments, Prayer-books, and little Sunday-school books, with a few Bibles. The sooner we get them the better; otherwise, you or he will be so good as to order a supply from the

Society for Promoting Christian Knowledge, to which I do not belong, or I would send for them. They may be directed to Park-street."

To Mrs. Carter she writes, "It is grievous to reflect, that while we are sending missionaries to India, our villages are in pagan darkness, and upon many of them scarcely a ray of Christianity has shone. I speak from the most minute and diligent examination. I have been constantly occupied for a long time in trying what my poor abilities and my small influence over others richer and better, can bring about. In one particular spot, for instance, there are six large parishes without so much as a resident curate. Through the kind assistance of a friend or two, I am endeavoring to fix schools and other little institutions in the most destitute of these places, and as they are from six to ten miles distant, you will judge that it employs a good deal of my time. I have the satisfaction to tell you that Cheddar, our first establishment, goes on prosperously. We have a great many children in that parish only, and by the ability and piety of our teachers, their improvement surpasses my warmest hopes. I make no apology to you, my dear friend, for the freedom of these details. Alas, there are so few to whom one can speak or write upon such subjects.

"Poor Patty is a great sufferer. Our friend Mrs. Garrick, who is still at Bristol Wells, has been to see us several times: she does not think herself quite recovered. To those who have enjoyed during a lifetime perfect health, illness is particularly alarming. Let you and me, my dear friend, number our infirm health among the merciful providences which have been dispensed to us. How much more do we enjoy our intervals of ease than those who know no pains; and I hope we may be able to turn the pain itself to a good account. 'All things work together for good to them that love God.'

"I wish you could see my roses. I have a double end in such a wish, for then I should see *you*. I am truly and faithfully, my dearest Mrs. Carter, yours."

At this time the elder sisters retired from their school, after a professional experience of nearly thirty years, highly creditable to themselves, and amply rewarded by an extensive patronage, which enabled them to build a fine house in Bath, and spend their later years in the enjoyment of every comfort which competency and piety can bestow.

The Mendip schools were dear to the sisterhood: each bore her share in their labors, fatigues, anxieties, and conflicts, sustaining and encouraging Hannah in the conspicuous and important part which her talents and energy awarded her.

In the establishment of these schools, the difficulties to be overcome needed all the resolution and judgment of minds like theirs. Though the field was in a land of Bibles and Sabbaths, yet a preparatory work, not unlike that which is necessary on heathen ground, was needed here; the people whom they wished to benefit, had to be *conciliated:* fearing not God, or regarding man, they neither desired nor cared for the blessings which Christian love would bestow: there were the prejudices and opposition of the small farmers, the hardness and guilt of the poor, the hatred of the ale-houses, the indifference of the church; a general ignorance and incapability of appreciating the nature of the good to be conferred upon them; the difficulty also of obtaining suitable teachers, prudent, discreet, and pious. 'Add to these," said Miss Hannah, after the good work was in progress, "the teaching of the teachers, which is not the least part of the work: having about thirty masters and mistresses, with under-teachers, one has continually to bear with the faults, the ignorance, the prejudices, humors, misfortunes, and *debts* of all these poor, well-meaning people. I hope, however, it teaches one forbearance, and it serves to put me in mind how much God has to bear from me. I now and then comfort Patty, in our journeys home at night, by saying, if we do these people no good, I hope we do some little good to ourselves."

But Miss More neither flinched nor faltered in her arduous service: she who had not hesitated to speak plain but unwelcome truths to the gay and great, would shrink from no personal fatigue, nor be disheartened either by opposition or indifference.

"For the first year," said Miss More, in speaking of the mother and daughter whom she had engaged as teachers for Cheddar—and the difficulties presented at Cheddar were like those of every other place where schools had been planted—"these excellent women had to struggle with every kind of opposition, so that they were frequently tempted to give up their laborious employ. They well entitled themselves to £30 per annum salary and some little presents. They visited the sick, chiefly with a view to their spiritual concerns; but we concealed the true motive at first: and in order to procure them access to the homes and hearts of the people, they were furnished not only with medicine, but with a little money, which they administered with great prudence. They soon gained their confidence, read and prayed to them, and in all respects did what a good clergyman does in other parishes.

"At the end of the year we perceived that much ground had been gained among the poor; but the success was attended with no small persecution from the rich, though some of them grew more favorable.

"I now ventured to have a sermon read after school on a Sunday evening, inviting a few of the parents, and keeping the grown-up children; the sermons were of the most awakening sort, and soon produced sensible effects. It was at first thought a very methodistical measure, and we got a few broken windows; but quiet perseverance, and the great prudence with which the zeal of our good mistresses was regulated, carried us through. Many reprobates were by the blessing of God awakened, and many swearers and Sabbath-breakers reclaimed. The number both of young and old scholars increased, and the daily life and conversation of many seemed to keep pace with their religious professions on the Sunday.

"We now began to distribute Bibles, Prayer-books, and other good books, but never at random, and only to those who had given some evidence of their loving and deserving them. They are always made the reward of superior learning, or some other merit, as we can have no other proof that they will be read. Those who manifest the greatest diligence, get the books of most importance. During my absence in the winter, a great many will learn twenty or thirty chapters, psalms, and hymns.

"Finding the wants and distresses of these poor people uncommonly great—for their wages are but one shilling per day—and fearing to abuse the bounty of my friends by too indiscriminate liberality, it occurred to me that I could make what I had to bestow go much further, by instituting clubs or societies for the women, as is done for the men in other places. It was no small trouble to accomplish this; for though the subscription was only three half-pence a week, it was more than they could always raise; yet the object appeared so important, that I found it would be good economy privately to give widows and other very poor women money to pay their club. After combating many prejudices, we carried this point, which we took care to involve in the general system, by making it subservient to the schools, the rules of the club restraining the women to such and such points of conduct respecting the schools. In some parishes we have one hundred and fifty poor women thus associated; you may guess who are the patronesses."

These clubs proved a great blessing to the little communities in which they were established, by helping the poor to husband their small resources for a time of need, and teaching them the importance and advantage of economy: in sickness, a member received three shillings a week; for lying-in, seven shillings and sixpence.

A girl trained in their schools and sustaining a virtuous character, was presented on her marriage-day with five shillings, a pair of white stockings, and a new Bible.

"Henceforth," says Miss More, "I desire

to have little to do with the great. I have devoted the remnant of my life to the poor and those that have no helper; and if I can do them no good, I can at least sympathize with them; and I know it is some comfort for a forlorn creature to be able to say, 'There is something that cares for me.' The simple idea of *being cared for* has always appeared to me a very cheering one; besides, the affection they have for me is a strong engine with which to lift them to a love of higher things. Alas, I might do more and better; pray for me."

When at Wrington, which now began to be the greater part of the year, accompanied by one of her sisters, usually Patty, she endeavored to visit at least three parishes every Sabbath, riding from ten to thirty miles, often enduring thirteen hours' exposure to the weather, and frequently passing the night at some of the villages, and all this for upwards of twenty years. What heroic devotion and inflexibility of purpose does this not reveal, at an age too when most women are too willing to retire from arduous labor in their Master's service, and beg to be excused from the call of Christian duty.

How beautiful among the cottages are the feet of her who bringeth glad tidings!

CHAPTER X.

NEWTON IN SORROW—MENDIP FEAST.

Mr. Newton is smitten, and he seeks the Christian sympathy of Hannah More. His wife, the idol of his early days, the companion of his later years, is no more.

"I could begin every letter," ran his, "with the words of David, 'Oh magnify the Lord with me, and let us exalt his name together.' Great has been his goodness. I am a wonder to many, and to myself. You perhaps know, madam, from what you have read of mine, and possibly from what you have seen in me, that my attachment to my dearest wife was great, yea excessive, yea idolatrous. It was so when it began. I think no writer of romance ever imagined more than I realized. It was so when I married. She was to me precisely—how can I write it?—in the place of God. In all places and companies my thoughts were full of her. I did every thing for her sake; and if she was absent—for I made three long voyages to Africa afterwards—I could take pleasure in nothing. So narrow were my notions of happiness at this time, that I had no idea that I was capable of any thing greater or better than of being always with her. By degrees, He who has the only right to my heart, and who alone can fill it, was pleased to make me sensible of his just claim, and my idol was brought some steps lower down; yet still I fear there was somewhat of the golden calf in my love, from the moment that joined our hands to the moment of separation. She was certainly my chief temporal blessing, and the providential hinge upon which all the principal events of my life have turned. Before I was four years old, she was sent into the world to be my companion, and to soften the rugged path of life. The difficulties in the way of our union were so many, so great, so apparently insuperable, that my hope of obtaining her seemed little less chimerical than if I had expected the crown of Poland. Yet at the proper time it took place. Fond as I was of her, I knew that inconstancy and mutability are primary attributes of the *human heart depraved*, if left to itself; but as the providence of God joined our hands, a secret blessing from him cemented our hearts. We certainly understood Thomson when he says,

> 'Enamored more as more remembrance swells
> With many a proof of recollected love.'

Further, though I had deserved to forfeit he: every day of my life, yet He spared her to me more than forty years; and lastly, which is the crowning mercy, when he recalled the loan—for, strictly speaking, she was not mine, but his—he made me willing to resign her. Through the long course of her very trying illness he supported me. Though my feelings were often painful, I believe a stranger who had seen me in company, or heard me from the pulpit, would hardly have suspected what was passing at home. On the evening of the 15th instant I watched her, with a candle in my hand, for some hours; and when I was sure she had breathed her last—which could not at once be determined, she went away so easily—I kneeled down by her bedside, with those who were in the room, and thanked the Lord, I trust with all my heart, for her dismission. I slept this night as well as usual; and in defiance of the laws of tyrant custom, I continued to preach while she lay dead in the house. We deposited her in our own vault on the 23d, and last Sunday evening I was enabled to preach her funeral sermon, from Habakkuk 3 : 17, 18.

"In writing to you I feel my heart open ; I am assured of meeting from you with that sympathy and sensibility of which I hope I am not myself wholly destitute; and therefore I will tattle on. This was not a sudden stroke. She did not die by a flash of lightning, by what is called accident, nor by those rapid disorders which break the thread of life in a few days or hours. The Lord gave me time to prepare for it; yea, by the gradual train of his dispensations, he gradually prepared me for it himself.

"She was confined to the house nearly ten years, excepting that in September, 1789, she was enabled to go for a month to Southampton, and during the last autumn went out every evening in a coach, for a little air. But she was shut up from the house of God, and from visiting her friends, though, till about September, she could generally receive them at home. Indeed, till about that time I did not give up all hope of her recovery. But a total loss of appetite, or rather, a loathing of food, then took place, which soon reduced her to a state of great weakness. In the beginning of October she took to her bed, and was soon after, I suppose from some defect in the spine, deprived of all locomotive power. She could neither move herself, nor without the greatest difficulty be moved—sometimes not so much as to have any thing about her changed for a fortnight together. Such, my dear madam, was the state of my idol: what a rebuke—what a lesson was it to me, to see her lie for eight or nine weeks in so sad and pitiable a situation! But the case was mingled with many merciful alleviations. Her patience was wonderful; her natural spirits as good as when she was in health. Often when my eyes were full of tears, she has constrained me to smile. When she could not move her body, she was thankful that she could move her hands, thankful that the Lord had laid no more upon her than she could bear; and when I once said, 'You are a great sufferer,' she replied, 'I do suffer, but not greatly.' So to know that we are sinners, and so to know the Saviour as to feel both the necessity and the liberty of applying to him, constitutes that knowledge which chiefly deserves the name; and this I trust was her privilege long before her last illness. But the enemy of our peace found advantage, from the weakness of her frame, to distress her with doubts which did not so directly apply to her own state as to the whole system of truth. She said, 'If there be a Saviour'—'If there be a God.' In this interval, which lasted near a fortnight, there was some abatement of that serenity I spoke of, some signs of impatience, and she discovered a strong reluctance to the thought of dying. Then was my sharpest trial; but the cloud gradually wore off, and for the last month she spoke of her departure with great composure, and seemed perfectly reconciled to it. Yet she never recovered strength and freedom to speak much to me about herself. The Sunday before she died, I said, 'If you cannot easily speak, and if your mind be at peace, I wish you to signify it by holding up your hand.' She immediately held it up, and waved it for a little time. This from her, who knew the gospel so well, comforted and satisfied me. It reminded me of the striking scene in Shakspeare, of Cardinal Beaufort, which closes with, 'He dies—but gives no sign.' Blessed be God, it was not her case.

"In the course of the day she asked for

me, though I was seldom long or far from her; but her head was so much affected by lying many weeks in one position, that though perfectly sensible, she could hardly bear the sound of the gentlest voice, or the softest footsteps upon the carpet. I went to her; she stroked my face, squeezed my hand, and said, 'My pretty dear!' an appellation she frequently gave me. We both dropped a few tears. These were the last words I heard her speak, and I could say but little. Such was our last farewell. From that night until she obtained her release, she gave little sign of life but by breathing.

"Now, my dear madam, I have done. I shall trouble you with no more in this strain. She is gone; and may I not add, I am going? For though my health was never better than at present, I am advancing in my sixty-sixth year. What is the world to me now? All the treasures of the Bank of England could not repair my loss, or even abate my sense of it. My chief earthly tie to this life is broken; yet I thank God I am willing to live while he has any service for me to do, or rather, while he pleases, whether I can serve him or not, provided I am favored with submission to his will.

I have lost my right hand. He has made me willing to part with it, but I must expect to miss it often. However, I thank him, I am by no means uncomfortable. I am satisfied he does all things well; and though some months ago, had it been lawful, I would have redeemed her life and health by the sacrifice of a limb, and thought the purchase cheap; yet now his will is made known by the event, I trust I can from the heart say with Fenelon, 'I would not take up a straw to have things otherwise than they are.' Time is short. A new and inconceivable scene will soon open upon us, and if they who now 'sow in tears shall reap in joy,' they may smile while they weep.

"We seem to want some other word by which to denote our supreme regard for God, than that which expresses our affection to creatures. When we speak of loving him, it must be in a different sense. Creature love is a passion; divine love is a principle. It arises from an apprehension of his adorable perfections, especially as they are displayed in the great work of redemption, without which it is impossible for a sinner to love him.

"There is a sensibility of feeling in creature love, which is no proper standard of our love to God. This, depending much upon condition and the state of the animal spirits, is different in different persons, and in the same persons at different times. It is variable as the weather, and indeed is often affected by the weather and a thousand local circumstances no more in our power than the clouds that fly over our heads. It is no uncommon thing to judge more favorably of ourselves on this point on a bright summer's day, and while contemplating a beautiful prospect, than in the gloom of winter, or the hurry of Cheapside. The high affection of some people may be compared to a summer's brook after a hasty rain, which is full and noisy for a little time, but soon becomes dry. But true divine love is like a river which always runs, though not always with equal depth and flow, and never ceases till it finds the ocean. The best evidences are, admiration of his way of saving sinners, humble dependence on his care, desire of communion with him in his instituted means of grace, submission to the will of his providence, and obedience to the dictation of his precepts. To keep his commandments, and to keep them as *His* commandments, from a sense of his authority and goodness, is the best, the most unsuspicious test of our love to Him."

A year after, Newton comes to Cowslip Green.

"Pray, my dear sir," wrote Miss More in a note which met him on the way, "try to divert your mind from the delights and elegances of Teston, before you turn your way towards my little thatched cottage, where a quiet cell, a few books, a maple dish, and a 'dinner of herbs' are all you can in reason expect; but then I hope we shall be able to furnish the appropriate sauce of 'quietness therewith,' for which I trust you will be contented to renounce the 'stalled ox' of noisy London."

He passed a week there in August—a week of Christian intercourse, the memory of which cheered him on his solitary pilgrimage.

In passing King Weston's hill, on his homeward journey, nothing in the wide and beautiful prospect delighted his eye like a glimpse of the Mendip Ridge: "Yes, yes, and I was so foolish as almost to envy a hill which, if it had eyes like me, might look at Cowslip Green from morning till night."

Nor is the interest dimmed by the dirt of Cheapside, or the duties of Colman-street.

"Every Sunday morning," he writes, "my thoughts set out in quest of you and Miss Patty, and though I know not what road you have taken, I seldom miss finding you. There is a communion of spirit among the believing members of that body of which Christ is the living head, which I believe is not impeded by local distance."

"I assure you," replied Miss More, "your kind wishes and your affectionate remembrance of the mountains of Mendip and of the little hermitage at the foot of it, are returned with great sincerity. Your pipe still maintains its station in the black-currant bush, and that hand would be deemed very presumptuous and disrespectful which should presume to displace it. For my own part, the pipe of Tityrus, though in my youthful days I liked it passing well, would not now be deemed a more venerable relic; and even the little sick maid Lizzy, who gratefully remembers the spiritual comfort you administered to her, often cries out, 'Oh dear, I hope nobody will break Mr. Newton's pipe.'

"Patty and I remember you as we are trotting over the hills. She desires her affectionate regards, as do all the rest. You would enjoy the vale of cowslips in this renewed spring: we have every thing of the golden age except the innocence; the garden is full of roses as in June, and an apple-tree is literally covered at the same moment with fruit nearly ripe and fresh blossoms."

In order to increase a general interest in the schools, and reward the punctual attendance of the scholars, the ladies busied themselves in preparing a feast, or what we should call a Sabbath-school picnic, the first of the kind perhaps ever held. The spot selected on this occasion was on one of the Mendip hills, eight miles from Cowslip Green, commanding a beautiful and varying prospect of the British channel and the Welsh mountains, with quiet hamlets in the foreground: the land was fenced in, tents pitched, and tables spread; children and teachers flocked to the spot at an early hour; a large party in wagons started from Cowslip Green, while the strangeness of the event attracted innumerable lookers-on without the enclosure. Psalms were sung, addresses made, and nine hundred sat down to a dinner of beef, plum pudding, and cider; all the neighboring clergy were present, and grace was said at each table; the day was fine, and

Miss Patty's fears speedily subsided before the good order and decorum which everywhere prevailed throughout this immense gathering. A general chorus of "God save the King" closed the festivities of the day, Miss More always inculcating loyalty in her code of religious duty.

The female clubs also had their anniversary days, when a sermon was preached at the parish church, and tea and cakes were served by the sisters at an adjoining school-room. These feasts, held from time to time, were attended with the most beneficial results, creating self-respect among the poor, and awakening stronger sympathy in their behalf among those who had power to benefit them.

A train of carriages, extending no less than a mile, frequently left Cowslip Green on such occasions, nor did the highest dignitaries in church or state disdain the thatched schoolhouses of Cheddar and Shipham.

On one pleasant summer's day, a gentleman came that way. "How beautiful is this," he said, stopping at the gate to survey the rural charms of Cowslip Green.

Miss Mary More issued from the shrubbery, and invited the stranger in.

Delighted with the situation and garden, he inquired to whom it belonged.

"Hannah More," was the reply.

His surprise only equalled his pleasure. An introduction followed, and Mr. Turner, for it was he, willingly became her guest.

Their long suspended intercourse was renewed, and remained unbroken until his death. He became a not unfrequent visitor at the cottage, and was a delighted spectator of the last picnic given by the ladies on the Mendip Ridge.

CHAPTER XI.

WILL CHIP AND HIS BRETHREN.

The angry clouds of revolution which swept over France during the latter part of the last century, began to darken the English horizon. The fond hopes awakened by the assembling of the States-general had long since been dissipated: in place of reform there was revolution; confusion and anarchy swiftly followed; opinions and principles hostile to order, government, and religion, were propagated under the guise of philosophy and fraternity, seducing the unwary by a promised good never to be realized. The clubs of France had overturned and overturned, until the throne, the state, the church, all civil, social, and moral law had been trampled down, and the bleeding people were left to the reckless fury of leaders who knew not God, neither regarded man. Wild as was this spirit of change, it swept over the English channel, gathering up the loose and discordant elements of the English masses, threatening the peace of society and the stability of the state.

As much of this agitation and discontent was grumbling in workshops, and muttering in ale-houses and clubs, and therefore beyond the reach of statesmen and below the cognizance of law, it must be met, if met at all, on its own ground, with its own weapons—English sense against French fraternity; tract and pamphlet against tract and pamphlet. Dr. Paley was enlisted in the service. He wrote "Reasons for Contentment," and a prebend of St. Paul's was his reward. The book aimed above the mark: it relieved the anxiety of a higher class, but did not quell the tumultuous hopes or answer the dangerous sophistry of the discontented and seditious. Something more direct and practical was wanted—somebody with quick wit and sound sense, who knew the men to be dealt with. At last, Will Chip showed himself to the English public. Will Chip, with no more than a sling and a few smooth stones, ventured forth to meet the Goliath of the times. Will Chip makes no boasts; he simply asks to be heard and read: he has written "Village Politics," a tract, very brief, and as everybody began to say, on reading it, very pertinent and very pithy. Bookseller Rivington issued it, and his shop is thronged, for wonderful is the demand for "Village Politics." Bishops christen it, lords bless it, landholders rejoice over it, everybody for law and order is thankful for it; it multiplies abundantly: one hundred thousand copies are circulated through lanes and courts; it speedily makes the circuit of the kingdom; it goes by hosts into Scotland and Ireland; it leaps into France, and passes into Italy; it is hawked and peddled; in hall and cottage "Village Politics" is known and read. Will Chip has proved himself a master-workman; he is thankful and contented, loyal and Christian, with a plenty of work to do, and a heart to do it. "What is a French Democrat," cries Will Chip, "but one who likes to be governed by a thousand tyrants, yet can't bear a king? And what is French equality, but every man trying to pull down every one that is above him; while, instead of raising those below him to his own level, he only makes use of them as steps to raise himself to the place of those he has tumbled down? and French philosophy, but to believe there is neither God nor devil, heaven nor hell? and French benevolence, but contempt of religion, aversion to justice, overturning of law, doubting all mankind in general, and hating everybody in particular? and as for equalization, fraternization, inviolability, it is nonsense, gibberish, downright hocus-pocus!"

Will Chip was a match for the times; and people said that his tact and intelligence did more than anybody's else to open the eyes of the people to the follies of French politics, and set Englishmen considering that, "though they had a king, he was so kept in, he could not hurt the people if he would; that they had as much liberty as could make them happy, more trade and riches than allowed them to be good; the best laws in the world, if they were more strictly enforced; and the best religion in the world, if it were but better followed."

Englishmen began to come to their senses, and acknowledge Will Chip told the truth. But who was this remarkable fellow, so shrewd, so pointed, so seasonable, so posted in "Village Politics" and French policy? Where did Will Chip live? The Bishop of London knew, for he writes to Mrs. Chip:

"I have this moment received your husband's Dialogue, and it is supremely excellent. I look upon Mr. Chip to be one of the finest writers of the age; this work alone will immortalize him; and what is better still, I trust it will help to immortalize the constitution. If the sale is as rapid as the book is good, Mr. Chip will get an immense income, and completely destroy all equality at once. How Jack Anvil and Tom Hod will *bear* this I know not, but I shall rejoice at Mr. Chip's elevation, and should be extremely glad at this moment to shake him by the hand, and ask him to take a family dinner with me. He is really a very fine fellow. I have kept your secret most religiously.

"Your very sincere and faithful

"B. LONDON."

But secrets, like murder, will out. Mrs. Boscawen suspects.

"Oh, Oh, say you so?" she writes to Hannah More. "It must have been *instinct* then that has made me send for a quarter of a hundred more of 'Will Chip,' and still for more and more; the last bale came in yesterday, and I see they will not last the week out; I had better have had a hundred at once. Last week I sent a packet to Badminton, and my duchess answers me thus: 'We have all read, and delight in your Village Politics.' A gentleman here says he shall send for a gross of them to distribute about in his neighborhood. I have not had a gross, to be sure, like this Gloucestershire gentleman, but I have had them past counting, little thinking—why, yes, I did think too of somebody, though not just the true body; for you must know the first word I ever heard of poor Tom Hod, or the sprightly consolations of his facetious neighbor Jack Anvil, was one night at Lady Cremorne's, where the Bishop of London pulled them out of his pocket, and read the delectable dialogue to us, in tones so suitable that he was interrupted continually with our bursts of laughter—ask Mrs. Kennicott else, for she was of the audience—and when he came to 'my lady,' and sent her 'to cold water, and hot water, and salt water, and fresh water,' he could not get on at all, we laughed so immoderately. I suspected his lordship was the author. 'Well,' as Tom says, I went home, and sure enough I wrote upon a bit of paper that minute, 'A quarter of a hundred of Will Chip, or Village Politics, to be had at Rivington's;' and this I gave to citizen Brown, and bid him carry it early next morning to a certain walking bookseller of mine, who procures me all the learning I deal in; and this was accordingly done, but did not hold me, as I said, three days; I have had many recruits since, and must have more. Last night a gentleman gave me 'Reasons for Contentment,' by Archdeacon Paley, addressed to the laboring part of the British public. I cast my eyes over it, and though I honor Archdeacon Paley, yet I assured the giver that I would send him the production of one, the minute I got home, who understood the language much better; and accordingly I despatched a little packet of Will Chip before I sat down at home. You will believe that I have not forgotten to supply Richmond. Our minister and our apothecary are supplied; and the first went to the house of Cambridge, and there excited envy, Mr. Cambridge declaring he wished he had written it. Mr. Rivington still dispenses them by thousands—I hope some go to France;—and though he cannot get any thing by them, nor the pleasant author, yet both will allow that this is success."

It was a new department for Hannah More; so influential and successful had she proved herself as a village politician, the Bishop of London besought her to come out on the side of religion and the Bible in "Village Christianity."

The pen of Miss More was not idle. If French politics had alarmed and nerved her to action, the unblushing confessions of French infidelity shocked her moral sense, and filled her with the most serious apprehensions.

"Dupont's and Manuel's atheistical speeches," writes she in April to Horace Walpole, now Earl of Oxford, "have stuck in my throat all the winter, and I have been waiting for our bishops and clergy to take some notice of them; but blasphemy and atheism have been allowed to become familiar to the minds of our common people, without any attempt being made to counteract the poison."

The attempt was, however, made by Miss More: "I know how paltry is the little I can do," she says, "but my conscience tells me that that little ought to be done."

Miss More's "Remarks on the Speech of M. Dupont," before the National Convention on Religion and Public Education, made its appearance in the spring, together with an address to the ladies of Great Britain in behalf of the French emigrant clergy; these exiles flocked to England in great numbers, extremely destitute, many lacking even the necessaries of life. To those in Bath, the sisters freely extended the hospitalities of their house, and a thousand pounds were raised through Hannah's influence in their behalf.

"Your work is so much above praise," writes Mrs. Montagu to her, "your mind so superior to vanity and a desire of fame, that I shall not repeat to you a word of the universal admiration it has excited, and the great approbation of the sentiments which prompted you to write it. I will barely assure you of what alone interests you, that this work will afford great assistance to the poor refugees, and will be of infinite service to the souls of thousands."

A sunny letter from the Bishop of London to the lady of Cowslip Green discourses thus:

"As you certainly belong to my diocese, and are on many accounts fairly entitled to the benefit of clergy—for you can not only read, but also write, and even preach to the great world more eloquently than most clergy-women—I cannot do very much amiss, I think, in sending you the enclosed charge. There are two things at least you will learn from it: to sing psalms more melodiously in your parish church, and to reside more constantly in your proper diocese, from which—as I know by experience—you are but too apt to wander, and to be led astray into the flowery paths of Cowslip, and such like seducing and dangerous places, where you forget, amid the dissipations of solitude, your duty towards your neighbor, and never think of bestowing one single solitary line on Mr. Walpole, or on me. I have lately received a letter from him, in which he complains most bitterly of your pertinacious silence. Pray let us hear soon how your cowslips and daisies and acacias go on, and how many tons of hay you have this year, for I take it for granted you are a great farmer.

"Your friend Lord Oxford and myself are, I believe, the only persons in the kingdom worthy of the hot weather, the only true, genuine summer we have had for the last thirty years; we both agreed that it was perfectly celestial, and that it was quite scandalous to huff it away as some people did. A few days before it arrived, all the world was complaining of the dreadfully cold north-east wind; and in three days after the warmer weather came in, everybody was quarrelling with the heat, and sinking under the rays of the sun. Such is that consistent and contented thing called human nature. As to ourselves, we enjoyed with gratitude and delight this truly Italian but short-lived summer. We lived in Bishop's noble northern room all the day, and in the evening the meadows were our drawing-room; there our little lawn was as green as an emerald, and kept constantly cool with fresh breezes from the Thames, while every other field and garden in the kingdom was burned up, and brought actually to the color of a gravel-walk. Our little cottage was indeed quite delicious, and this summer alone has amply repaid me for all my trouble and expense."

Great as was the care and labor of superintending the Cheddar schools, Miss More still projected new plans for the improvement and elevation of the laboring classes. There was, at that period, a great lack of reading sufficiently cheap, lively, and instructive, to be within the range of their means and tastes. Hannah More asked, "How can this deficiency be supplied?" In the unsettled, discontented, and inquiring state of the English masses, it seemed imperiously necessary to furnish them with the right sort of reading: if Will Chip had done good service by his judicious efforts in Village Politics, might he not labor with equal efficiency for temperance, economy, religion, social stability, and moral improvement?

Miss More thought he might: at least, the attempt was worth making; and this gave rise to "The Cheap Repository," a monthly publication, cheap enough to come within the means of the humblest cottager.

"Thank you a thousand times for your most ingenious plan," exclaimed the Earl of Oxford. "May great success reward you. How calm and comfortable must your slumbers be on the pillow of every day's good deeds!" Patty and Sarah, with other friends, promised their assistance, and the work was happily commenced. Two committees were formed in London to promote its regular circulation, and two millions were sold the first year.

In the winter of the year 1794, which had been almost unremittingly occupied in work among her schools, with her pen, or in lesser schemes of active usefulness, she journeyed to London, and paid a few visits among old friends.

"Last Saturday I dined with Mrs. Montagu. It was almost two years since I had found myself in such *grande monde;* so I told them if I should be caught doing any thing vulgar, they must give me a jog. We were fourteen at dinner, and many more were added after, most of them my old and intimate friends, who seemed to receive me with great kindness. I told them to make much of me, for their opportunities of seeing such a rarity would be few. Mrs. Montagu is well, bright, and in full song, and had spread far and wide the fame of Cowslip Green, and the day she passed there. In the midst of all the splendor of lights and grandeur and luxury, word was brought in of the death of poor Lady E——. It was a tremendous warning: she was an amiable, generous, and charitable woman, but was immersed in luxury and splendor.

"I went to Mrs. Boscawen, with whom I shall make a point to pass all the time I can spare. We have had many hours' quiet discussion. She is better, but I fear breaking up.

"Three o'clock. Called down to Mr. Henry Thornton, just arrived from Clapham, where he, Mr. Wilberforce, and Mr. Elliott have been quietly enjoying themselves several days. We have had two or three hours' prate, but our spirits were not exhausted: he is not in very stout health. Yesterday I went to hear

Mr. Cecil—Naaman the Syrian—very excellent."

March. "Dined with friends at Mrs. ——'s. 'What doest thou here, Elijah?' Felt too much pleased at the pleasure expressed by so many accomplished friends, on seeing me again. Keep me from contagion."

Sunday. "I see the need of doing the duty of every day in *its* day. When I look back on the past week, I see cause of mourning over my vanity and folly. Sloth and self are getting strong dominion, and much time wasted which I had devoted to improvement. Let these continual discoveries make me humble."

May. "Came to Fulham to my dear bishop: much kindness—literary and elegant society; but the habits of polished life, even of virtuous and pious people, are too relaxing. Much serious reading, but not a serious spirit; good health, with increased relaxation of mind: thus are the blessings of God turned against himself."

Some of Miss More's best efforts appeared in the pages of The Cheap Repository. The Shepherd of Salisbury Plain, originally one of its Sunday Tracts, will alone immortalize her.

In consequence of the political distractions

of the Continent, and the war which England was called upon to wage, together with the extreme severity of the weather in 1795, which cut off the crops, there was great suffering among the lower classes; cold, scarcity, and discontent everywhere prevailed. The Cheap Repository, with wonderful sagacity, furnished plans and precepts for enabling the people to bear the ills which pressed thus heavily upon them, and inculcated religious truths in so simple and direct a manner, that the faith of multitudes, shaken by the shallow sophistries of infidelity, became strengthened in the good old ways of their fathers.

Illustrious was the race of Chips. Mrs. Jones' cheap dishes in "Hester Wilmot" were in repute even at the tables of the rich; "Black Giles the Poacher" frightened everybody trying to live by their wits rather than their work; no temperance agent ever effected more good than "Sorrowful Sam;" while the "Riot" ballad, seasonably sung among a gang of miners on the eve of a rising, saved the mills, spared the butchers, and restored quiet to a most seditious neighborhood.

Bishop Butler's Analogy for a half-penny is surely worthy of record; the doubts, perplexities, and sinful grumblings of many a one careful and troubled about many things, are happily and sensibly rebuked in this most excellent epitome of one of the grand truths of God's providential government: no one can read "Turn the Carpet" without having his faith confirmed, and whether willing to confess it or not, being ashamed of envious comparisons and ungrateful murmurs.

TURN THE CARPET, OR THE TWO WEAVERS.

IN A DIALOGUE BETWEEN DICK AND JOHN.

As at their work two weavers sat,
Beguiling time with friendly chat,
They touched upon the price of meat,
So high, a weaver scarce could eat.

"What with my brats and sickly wife,"
Quoth Dick, "I 'm almost tired of life;
So hard my work, so poor my fare,
'T is more than mortal man can bear.

"How glorious is the rich man's state!
His house so fine, his wealth so great!
Heaven is unjust, you must agree;
Why all to him? why none to me?

"In spite of what the Scripture teaches,
In spite of all the parson preaches,
This world—indeed, I 've thought so long—
Is ruled, methinks, extremely wrong.

"Where'er I look, howe'er I range,
'T is all confused and hard and strange;
The good are troubled and oppressed,
And all the wicked are the blessed."

Quoth John, "Our ign'rance is the cause
Why thus we blame our Maker's laws:
Parts of his ways alone we know;
'T is all that man can see below.

"Seest thou that carpet, not half done,
Which thou, dear Dick, hast well begun?
Behold the wild confusion there;
So rude the mass it makes one stare!

"A stranger, ign'rant of the trade,
Would say, No meaning 's there conveyed;
For where 's the middle, where 's the border?
Thy carpet now is all disorder."

Quoth Dick, "My work is yet in bits,
But still in every part it fits.
Besides, you reason like a lout;
Why, man, that *carpet's inside out*."

Says John, "Thou say'st the thing I mean,
And now I hope to cure thy spleen:
This world, which clouds thy soul with doubt,
Is but a carpet inside out.

"As when we view these shreds and ends,
We know not what the whole intends;
So when on earth things look but odd,
They 're working still some scheme of God.

"No plan, no pattern can we trace;
All wants proportion, truth, and grace:
The motley mixture we deride,
Nor see the beauteous upper side.

"But when we reach that world of light,
And view those works of God aright,
Then shall we see the whole design,
And own the Workman is divine.

"What now seem random strokes, will there
All order and design appear;
Then shall we praise what here we spurned,
For then the *carpet shall be turned.*"

"Thou 'rt right," quoth Dick; "no more I'll grumble
That this sad world 's so strange a jumble;
My impious doubts are put to flight,
For my own carpet sets me right."

CHAPTER XII.

TRIALS AND OPPOSITION.

IN June, Wilberforce made a bridal journey to Cowslip Green; Miss More willingly left the splendors of London to come and bid him welcome. "By this coming," she says, "he prepaid a sort of vow, made many years since; you will think it not amiss to make his agreeable wife set out with such an act of humility."

On the following Sunday, in company with the sisters, he visited the schools of Shipham, Axbridge, and Cheddar. Cheddar then was not the Cheddar of his first visit, eight years before, when the sight of its ignorant and wretched population robbed him of the pleasure of his trip. Wilberforce rejoiced, and thanked God for the blessed change.

This year, 1797, was marked by his marriage and the printing of his "Practical Christianity," for it had long been before the world in a life of practical godliness, known and read by all men. Practical Christianity was at a low ebb; there was little or no demand for books of that kind, and his friends tried to dissuade him from publishing it.

"If you put your name to it, you may possibly sell five hundred copies," said his bookseller, looking as if he thought that extremely doubtful. But the hidden want was little understood: a religious book of *its* nature and spirit was needed; and when issued, the demand was so great that a few days exhausted the edition.

"I am truly thankful to Providence," says the excellent Bishop Porteus, "that a work of this nature has made its appearance at this tremendous moment. I pray God it may have a powerful and extensive influence upon the hearts of men, and in the first place upon my own, which is already humbled, and will, I trust, in time be sufficiently humbled by it." "Such a book at such a time, and by such a man!" exclaims Newton: "I accept it as a token of good, yea, as the brightest token I can discern in this dark and perilous day."

Fifteen editions issued from the English press; twenty-five were sold in this country, and it took a high place among the instrumentalities that gave a quickened impulse to that warm and more earnest piety which has distinguished the last half century.

While Wilberforce visits Cowslip Green, and joins the sisters in their walks of usefulness, Newton enjoys their society and sympathy as fancy sketches them in the quiet of his study, or along the dust and din of Cheapside. "I am gone to the Vale of Mendip," writes he, "to Cowslip Green, to the Root house, where perhaps the ladies are just now assembled to breakfast. Oh, could I actually see them, with what glee should I say, 'Good morning, ladies!"

"Well, I must be content with ideal visits for the present, but not always; a day is approaching when we hope to have a joyful meeting indeed. I trust that Cowslip Green is holy ground, and all the inhabitants consecrated persons; sprinkled, like the priests of old, with the atoning blood, anointed with the holy unction, and devoted with united hearts, hands, and tongues, to do the will and to proclaim the praise of our God and Saviour. It is no wonder that I so long to be with them.

"Indeed, I am with you in spirit, and I think this is more than a sally of the imagination; the communion of saints, which we profess to believe, like the communion of the members of the body, is derived from a communication of life and spirits from the same common Head, by which they have reciprocal fellowship and fellow-feeling among themselves: and though believers, the salt of the earth, are scattered up and down, far and wide, to preserve the whole mass from putrefaction, they are *one* in Him. The supreme object of their love is as yet unseen. For his sake they love all who love him, though it is but few of them comparatively that they can expect to see, until he shall collect them together in the great day of his appearance. The virtue of the heavenly magnet which draws them all to himself, connects them at the same time with each other. Their aims, their hopes, and their spiritual sustenance are the same. Local distance neither discourages their mutual prayers, nor prevents their efficacy.

"The shadows of evening are advancing upon me. If ever I see Mendip again, it must be by a bird's-eye view from the higher hill of Zion above. But I trust I shall at intervals recollect with pleasure the happy week I passed at Cowslip Green while I can remember any thing."

The New-year's day of 1798 was solemnized by Hannah More by a renewed and more entire dedication of herself to the service of her heavenly Master. "Let me now give myself away with a more entire surrender than I have ever yet made," she records.

"1. I resolve, by the grace of God, to be more watchful over my temper.

"2. Not to speak idly or harshly.

"3. To watch over my thoughts; not to indulge in vain, idle, resentful, impatient, worldly imaginations.

"4. To strive after closer communion with God.

"5. To let no hour pass without lifting up my heart to him, through Christ.

"6. Not to let a day pass without some thought of death.

"7. To ask myself every night, when I lie down, Am I fit to die?

"8. To labor to do and to suffer the whole will of God.

"9. To cure my overanxiety by casting myself on God in Christ.

"I resolve to pray at least twice a week, separately, for the country in this time of danger, independently of the petitions offered up in my other prayers.

"Lord, grant that my religious advantages may never appear against me. Many temptations this week to vanity; flattery without end. God be praised, I was *not* flattered: twenty-four hours' headache makes me see the vanity of all this. Am I tempted to vanity? Let me recall to mind the shining friends I have lost this year, eminent each in his different way, yet he that is least in the kingdom of heaven is greater than either."

Among these shining friends was Horace Walpole, whose twenty years of unclouded kindness and pleasant correspondence Miss More could not drop without a sigh.

As the best proof of her sincerity, we find her this year extending her labors, and establishing a new school at Wedmore, the largest parish in the county, and deplorably ignorant. In the undertaking she met with unnumbered trials. The farmers were angry at her interference, and more hostile than any which the sisters had encountered before. In remodelling a damp and unfinished building for a school-house, she took a violent cold, which threw her upon a sick-bed. Though harassed and opposed, she went bravely on: it was enough for her to know that the work was to be done, and that Providence seemed to have appointed her to do it.

In the midst of her labors Wilberforce came from Bath, and carried her there to take the benefit of the waters.

"I feel it rather base to steal away and leave poor Patty to work double tides," she wrote to Mrs. Kennicott. "We have in hand a new and very laborious undertaking; but the object appeared to me so important that I did not feel myself at liberty to neglect it.

"The opposition I have met with in endeavoring to establish an institution for the religious instruction of these people would excite your astonishment: in spite of it, however, which far exceeds any thing which I have met with, I am building a house and taking up things on such a large scale, that you must not be surprised if I get into debt. Providence, I trust, will carry me through the undertaking; for, notwithstanding the active malevolence we experience, I have brought already three or four hundred under a course of instruction. The worst part of the story is, that thirty miles there and back is a little too much these short days; and when we get there, our house has neither windows nor doors: but if we live till next summer things will mend, and in so precarious a world as this is, a winter was not to be lost."

Besides these active duties, her pen was busily employed in preparing "Strictures on Female Education," which appeared in the beginning of the following year.

The tendencies then, as now, were towards amusement rather than sobriety, fashionable accomplishments instead of valuable knowledge and practical industry, filial independence in place of filial obedience.

The practical evils which lie in the path of Christian education, from low and imperfect notions of what should be its chief aim, together with a false estimate of worldly advantages, are portrayed with vigor and truth.

Her pertinent question to the women of her own time, may be asked with no less significance to ours, "Does it seem to be the true end of education to make women dancers, singers, players, painters, actresses, sculptors, gilders, varnishers, engravers, and embroiderers?

"Most men are commonly destined to some profession, and their minds are consequently turned each to its respective object. Would it not be strange if they were called out to exercise their profession or set up their trade with only a little general knowledge of the trades and professions of all other men, and without any previous definite application to their own peculiar calling? The profession of ladies to which the bent of their instruction should be turned, is that of daughters, wives, mothers, and mistresses of families. They should be, therefore, trained with a view to these several conditions, and be furnished with a stock of ideas and principles and qualifications and habits ready to be applied and appropriated, as occasion may demand, to each of these respective situations. For though the arts which merely embellish must claim admiration, yet when a man of sense comes to marry, it is a companion whom he wants, and not an artist. It is not merely a creature who can paint, and play, and sing, and draw, and dress, and dance; it is a being who can comfort and counsel him: one who can reason and reflect, and feel and judge, and discourse and discriminate; one who can assist him in his affairs, lighten his cares, strengthen his principles, and educate his children.

"Almost any ornamental acquirement is a good thing when it is not the *best* thing a woman has; and talents are admirable when not made to stand proxy for virtues."

May not much of the want of success, the failures, the bankruptcy, the discouragements, the complaints of men in business, be traced to a wrong domestic education? Are women sufficiently trained for a thorough understanding of their household duties? Do not fashionable accomplishments usurp the place of domestic virtues? Turn which way we can, gild and ornament, and reason and sentimentalize as we may, life is full of practical evils, unwrought materials, and sore trials, which require an earnest purpose, a patient, courageous heart, and skilful hands to convert them into present benefit or future good.

Miss More's happy criticism upon the word "pleasant," may not be amiss for the benefit of those who value entertainment at the expense of excellence.

"There was a time when a variety of epithets were thought necessary to express various kinds of excellence, and when the different qualities of the mind were distinguished by appropriate and discriminating terms:

when the words, venerable, learned, sagacious, profound, acute, pious, worthy, ingenious, valuable, elegant, agreeable, wise, or witty, were used as specific marks of distinct characters. But the legislators of fashion have of late years thought proper to comprise all merit in one established epithet—an epithet which, it must be confessed, is a very desirable one as far as it goes. This term is exclusively and indiscriminately applied wherever commendation is intended. The word *pleasant* now seems to combine and express all moral and intellectual excellence. Every individual, from the gravest professors of the gravest profession, down to the trifler who is of no profession at all, must earn the epithet of pleasant or must be contented to be nothing; and must be consigned over to ridicule under the vulgar and inexpressive cant word of *bore*. This is the mortifying designation of many a respectable man, who, though of much worth and ability, cannot perhaps clearly make out his letters-patent to the title of *pleasant*. For according to this modern classification there is no intermediate state, but all are comprised within the ample bounds of one or the other of these two comprehensive terms."

Her chapter upon Children's Balls, which she declares are a triple conspiracy against the innocence, health, and happiness of children, would be likely to give almost as much offence now as it did then. The remark of a Christian mother in one of our cities, that "the increasing prevalence of evening dancing parties and late hours for young children, she could not but consider a serious evil, yet felt obliged to yield to the fashion," reveal a sad defection in parental discipline which it is to be feared is gaining ground in the religious community.

The "Strictures" were greatly commended; letters of thanks, congratulation, encouragement, and praise poured in upon the author from the old circle, Mrs. Boscawen, Mrs. Montagu, Mrs. Chapone, Miss Carter, Mrs. Barbauld, and from many others less familiar to these pages.

The sisters Hannah and Patty now went up to London for the benefit of a change, to both mind and body. Mrs. Boscawen was extremely feeble at this time: "God bless you, my dear madam," said Hannah, on coming away, afraid lest it might be the last meeting.

"That is well," said the venerable lady,

taking her by the hand, and looking steadfastly into her face, "that is well, but you must do more, you must pray for me; I am going gently off."

Miss Carter at eighty-three was in the enjoyment of better health and spirits than usually fall to the lot of so advanced age, and the conversation of the friends, if less sparkling, savored more of Christian hope and holy joy.

Meanwhile troubles were brewing in one of her parishes, which proved extremely vexatious and distressing to Miss More and her family: viewed through the lapse of years, it seems strange that charges so inconsistent with truth could have been made against her, and that the affair could ever have assumed the dignity of a "controversy."

A school had been established in the profligate parish of Blagdon, near Cowslip Green, at the earnest and repeated request of both curate and magistrate, for Miss More, on their first application, felt that she had neither strength nor means for any new undertaking: having consented, she paid particular attention to its welfare, and in a few years had the satisfaction of knowing that disorders, warrants, and indictments had almost entirely disappeared before the benign and beneficial influence of the enterprise. For five years affairs went smoothly on, when one of her schoolmasters named Young was charged by the curate Mr. Bere with introducing Methodism into his school, which simply consisted in encouraging extemporaneous prayer, and speaking upon religious experience in a little meeting of a dozen poor neighbors. For this irregularity, as it was regarded, Miss More, who was then sick at Bath, gave him a timely reprimand, and the school went quietly on. Whether owing to some private pique or personal dislike, the curate was not so easily satisfied; he began to preach against the schools, and brought fresh accusations against the schoolmaster. The matter was referred to the rector, and afterwards to a local tribunal, the result of which was the dismissal of the schoolmaster and the disbanding of the school. Miss More acquiesced for peace' sake, though her judgment did not sanction the course. Young had been in her service for ten years, and his exemplary conduct and faithful discharge of duty had won a confidence not to be easily shaken. She recommended him to the patrons of a large charitable institution near Dublin.

who not long afterwards appointed him superintendent, the duties of which he fulfilled with credit to himself and to the satisfaction of his employers.

Disbanding the school cost her many struggles. "It is with no small concern I have to inform you that we shall meet no more in this place," she said in her parting address to the little flock who sat around her with anxious looks and tearful eyes. "The Sunday-school, and the evening reading, the weekly school of industry, are all at an end. Before we part, it is but justice to you to declare that my sister and I have never had more comfort from the teachable and dutiful behavior of any children, nor more satisfaction from the sober and decent conduct of any parents, than we have experienced in this place. You will give the best evidence that you have profited by our instructions and those of your master,. by carrying the religion you have been taught on Sunday into the business of the week and the behavior of your daily life. I shall hold that person's religious profession very cheap indeed, who is not hereafter sober, peaceable, industrious, and forgiving. Be diligent in your attendance at church twice a day. Show that you fear God, by keeping his commandments and reverencing his ministers; show that you 'honor the king,' by submitting to all that are in authority under him, especially to magistrates. Mr. Young has proved himself, during eight years' service, an honest and upright man, and an able and faithful schoolmaster. You are greatly indebted to him, and can reward him in no other way but by living in such a manner as shall be a credit to his instructions. He will continue in this place, of which he is a parishioner, till he can settle himself elsewhere; but I earnestly request that, though you treat him as a kind friend and neighbor, you do not, either by many or by few, resort to him for instruction.

"Young men, let me exhort you to be sober-minded; avoid the snares and corruptions of the world, against which you have been so long guarded, and to which, at your season of life, you will be so much exposed. My young women, so long the objects of our tender care and concern, I commit you to the protection of God. He can, and I trust he will raise up better friends than we have been to you. In any case he will himself be your friend, if you walk in the paths in which you have been trained. He will never leave you nor forsake you. As those hours on Sunday evenings which you have been accustomed to pass in this house are the seasons of the greatest dangers to your youth and ignorance, watch well, I beseech you, over yourselves. You are now furnished with Bibles; you have been taught to read and understand them; so that if you now fall into sin, you will no longer have the former excuse of ignorance to plead. We have this day repeated our annual gift of forty Bibles and Common Prayer books, the usual number of Bishop Gartrell's 'Institutes,' Bishop Beveridge's 'Private Thoughts,' Doddridge's 'Rise and Progress of Religion,' for the elder, with some hundreds of Cheap Repository and other small tracts for younger ones. To the use of these you must add prayer to God for his grace and direction. Though what little we have done here is mixed with much imperfection, yet I trust the general design and tendency of it has been right.

"We shall never think of the five years that are past without being thankful for what has been done, and without wishing we had done more and better. To the principal farmers and heads of the parish we are obliged for their approbation and countenance of the school, and their kindness to the master and mistress. Being willing to leave a last testimony of our regard to the poor, we have deposited in the hands of your respectable church-warden five guineas, to be applied to a general subscription, in case the scarcity should make such a measure necessary, or otherwise to be disposed of at his direction and that of the vestry."

The rector having learned that the schoolmaster's offence had never been repeated after Miss More's reprimand, dismissed Mr. Bere from the curacy, and requested Miss More to reopen the schools: this request was warmly seconded by her own affectionate interest in the little Blagdon flock, and accordingly she did so. But the curate was not so easily shaken off. Having committed no ecclesiastical or moral offence, he could not be deprived of his office, and he remained at Blagdon a thorn in her side. To disarm his hostility, in August she again closed the schools, not to be reopened.

Grieved and wounded to the quick, Hannah writes to Wilberforce, "In Blagdon is still a voice heard, lamentation and mourning; and at Cowslip Rachel is still weeping for her children, and refusing to be comforted because they are not instructed. This heavy blow has almost bowed me to the ground. It was only last night I began to get a little sleep. My reason and my religion know that it is permitted by that gracious Being who uses sometimes bad men for his instruments; but reason and religion do not operate much upon the nerves. I doubt not but that He who can bring much real good out of much seeming evil, will eventually turn this shocking business to his glory."

Hitherto we have only seen Hannah More borne on favoring gales; her London acquaintance rejoiced in her society and celebrity; fame and friends followed her to Cowslip Green; her home missionary labors, difficult and arduous as they had been, were crowned with success; her works placed her among the revered and honored of England: prosperity, we know, is neither favorable to piety nor self-knowledge, and the hour of trial came.

"If it please God," she says, "thus to put an end to my little—how little!—usefulness, I hope to be enabled to submit to his will; not only to submit to it because I cannot help it, but to *acquiesce in it, because it is holy, just, and good.*"

Though her reputation, her character, her labors were seemingly at stake—for the affair took the shape of a bitter quarrel, in which the sisters were assailed with personal abuse and public misrepresentation—no words of anger or recrimination or sinful repining issue from her lips. Conscious of her innocence as far as regards her fellow-men, she offers neither defence nor exculpation: her chief desire is spiritual improvement, an increased purity of heart, and a more humble reliance upon the Lord her strength.

"'Blessed are ye when men revile you and persecute you, and say all manner of evil against you *falsely*,' and 'for my name's sake.' When I consider whose words are these," wrote Newton to his afflicted friend, "I am more disposed to congratulate than to condole with you on the unjust and hard treatment that you have met with.

"Yet I do feel for you. These things are not joyous but grievous at the time; it is *afterwards* that they yield the peaceable fruits of righteousness. Cheer up, my friend; tarry thou the Lord's leisure. Be strong, and he shall comfort thy heart."

Among the charges laid against Miss More in this controversy, were those of teaching Calvinism, sympathizing with the Methodists, and encouraging dissenters. Though firmly attached to her church, Miss More was less a church woman than a Christian.

"*Bible* Christianity is what I love," said she, "that does not insist upon opinions indifferent in themselves—a Christianity practical and pure, which teaches holiness, humility, repentance, and faith in Christ; and which, after summing up all the evangelical graces, declares that the greatest of these is charity."

No better description than this could be given of her religious character: it grew out of large, intelligent, experimental views of *Bible* Christianity. No other Christianity but that which is drawn directly from the pure word of God can give equal symmetry and comprehensiveness—can blend in such just proportion the deepest self-abasement and the most trusting faith with the greatest amount of usefulness and good works.

CHAPTER XIII.

BARLEY WOOD.

VISITORS without number flocked to Cowslip Green, until Cowslip Green was too strait for the fame and hospitality of its mistress. She now projected a new house, more ample and commodious, upon a swell of land half a mile from Wrington, commanding a wider sweep of hill and valley, of hamlet and green. Its peculiar beauty led one of her friends to call it "the gift of an all-wise Providence, to soothe her after her troubles."

In conducting this new enterprise, Miss More hoped to regain that tranquillity of mind and strength of body which the trials she had passed through had seriously damaged.

Barley Wood became her residence in 1801.

Hitherto the sisters had divided their time between Bath and Wrington: they now determined to give up the care and expense of a divided dwelling and a bustling town, and spend the remainder of their days together at Barley Wood.

"Lord, grant that this prove a blessing to us all, and draw us nearer to him," exclaims Hannah; "make us thankful that our lot has fallen in so pleasant a place, that we have a goodly heritage; but let us not take up with so poor a portion as this life, or any thing in it."

Each sister has her place in the household. There sits Miss Mary, already past sixty, plain in manners and pointed in speech, who allows herself no indulgences, nor suffers any impropriety to pass without rebuke. Here is the *wife* of Barley Wood, Miss Elizabeth, gentle and loving; her presence, like a good angel, regulating, smoothing, harmonizing; and her work-basket, like Dorcas', filled with coats and garments for the poor. Miss Sally is bright and spicy. "Prosy More" she was called by intimates, in distinction from Hannah, who was sometimes dubbed "Poetry." Sarah was the author of two novels, and her witty repartees were the delight of friends, who declared her a living contradiction of Solomon's position, "nothing new under the sun."

The star of the sphere is Hannah: she is world-known now, and everybody comes to do her honor. There are lines of suffering upon her face, yet it is beaming with benevolence; the pressure of sickness is often heavy, but her elastic spirit seldom yields: she thinks and plans and works and reads even on the sick-bed.

On her first entrance to the new home, she was confined to her chamber, and "this puts me in mind," she says, "of the old remark, that the first spot of earth of which Abraham took possession in the land of promise, was a grave!"

Among the children of England who were sporting in her stately halls, one little girl there was on whose fair head rested a nation's hopes. She was remembered at every household altar; wise men talked of her, and good men prayed for her.

To the loyal heart of Hannah More, the education of the Princess Charlotte could hardly fail to be deeply interesting. Nor is it surprising that this gifted teacher should be asked to furnish, from the rich stores of her experience, valuable suggestions to those who had the charge of it.

To this end she wrote "Hints towards Forming the Character of a Young Princess," dedicated to Dr. Fisher, Bishop of Exeter, who had just been appointed preceptor to the royal pupil. Copies were presented to the king and queen, the prince and princess, who all alike bore testimony to its excellence. Not having a speedy introduction to this country, she understood it was excluded by our republican principles. When informed it was actually in circulation, much gratified, she exclaimed, "I have conquered America."

On the 7th of January, 1804, among the particular mercies which crowned her days, she enumerated, "considerable restoration of my health and spirits; personal and family comforts continued; family misfortunes averted; opportunities of doing some good; our schools continued; kindness of friends; ability to enjoy my sweet place; escape from the turbulent life of Bath; increased opportunities of reading and retirement," for which she desires to have an abiding and lively gratitude: "though for all earthly blessings we should pray only with entire submission to the divine will; while in praying for spiritual blessings, no reserve, no caution, no limit is necessary."

"Lord, pour out the grace of thy Holy Spirit on me and mine without measure; teach us to love thee with *all* our hearts, minds, souls, and strength, and to devote the remainder of our lives to thy service, and to the glory of our Lord and Saviour Jesus Christ."

This month closed her correspondence with Mrs. Boscawen.

"Yes, my very excellent and dear friend," wrote Mrs. Boscawen in her last letter, "I must send one word sooner or later, in return for the kindest of letters, which was a cordial to me; that one word must express the truest gratitude for such remembrance, the most constant affection, and the sincerest satisfaction in the news of your better health; so happily provided for by your own wisdom and activity, in removing from the vale below, and planting yourself so delightfully on a hill.

"I desire the continuance of your prayers for me, my dear friend; for Oh, what is it to live so long! It is, you will answer, the will of Him 'in whom we live and move and have our being.'

"Mrs. Carter was taken ill while dining with Mrs. Iremonger, but is better to-day. Adieu, my dear friend."

Mrs. Boscawen died soon after, and bequeathed forty volumes of the Port Royal authors to increase the library of her friend, and recall the memory of early days.

Sickness again visited Barley Wood, and for a year Miss More seemed hovering on the confines of the grave; it was a period of sorrowful suspense to her friends. Anxious inquiries were daily made at the gate, and prayers for her recovery arose from many a humble roof: nor was this solicitude confined to the cottage homes which had been comforted by her bounty and lighted by her instructions; every post brought letters of inquiry and sympathy, and at last all fears were put to rest by returning health.

Cheddar at this time sustained a severe loss by the death of its excellent curate, a faithful coadjutor of the sisters in their labors of love, whose plain preaching and pious life were greatly blessed to the people of his charge.

"You would weep over Cheddar," said Miss More to Wilberforce, "if you saw the change occasioned by the death of Drewitt: no resident minister, only a galloper from Wells on Sunday, to a twelve minutes' sermon; of course the meeting thins."

The great object to which Wilberforce had devoted the prime of his life and the strength of his manhood was now on the eve of completion. Slowly and steadily had the cause of the abolition of the slave-trade gained upon the English conscience. In spite of defeats, distrust, and discouragements without number, the London Committee, after an interval of seven years, reassembled in Palace-yard, strong with the strength of a noble cause. Wilberforce wrote a powerful appeal upon the Enormities of the Slave-trade, and every agency which could be brought into action was marshalled for the approaching crisis.

On the 22d of February, the first reading of the bill took place before the House of Lords. It was a night of exciting fear and hope. The vote stood 72 to 28.

"O Lord, let me praise thee with my whole heart!" ejaculates Wilberforce.

The House of Commons is grappling with it on the 23d.

Men spoke boldly for justice and humanity: they are earnest, and who shall gainsay them? The opposition was feeble and loose.

One of the members called upon men that day to mark how much the rewards of virtue were superior to those of ambition; to contrast the feelings of Napoleon in his greatness with those of the honored individual who should that night lay his head upon the pillow, and remember that through his agency the slave-trade was no more. Every eye was directed towards Wilberforce, and a sudden burst of applause rang through the House.

The vote stood 283 to 16. A month afterwards it came for a third reading before the House of Lords: two days afterwards, March 25, 1807, the bill received the royal sanction and became a law.

"Oh, what thanks do I owe the Giver of all good, for bringing me in his gracious providence to this great cause, which at length, after nineteen years of labor, is successful!" exclaims the master-spirit of the occasion.

"To speak of fame and glory to Mr. Wilberforce, would be to use language far beneath him," said Sir James Mackintosh. "How precious is time! How noble and sacred is human nature, made capable of achieving such truly great exploits."

"What a promise of happiness does it bear to millions and hundreds of millions of our species," wrote Mr. Stephens, the husband of Miss Wilberforce, to Hannah More, "and from what a load of odious guilt and shame does it deliver our country!"

We may well believe it a day of rejoicing at Barley Wood.

Bishop Porteus, the friend and coadjutor of both Wilberforce and Miss More, was nearing the end of his long and useful life. After his eye had become dim and his natural force abated he visited Barley Wood, and spent a few days with its gifted mistress.

Similarity of taste and character seems early to have drawn them together; she was a frequent guest at Fulham palace, where his sweetness of temper, playful wit, and innocent cheerfulness delighted the society of his more intimate friends, while he exercised the functions of his high office with zeal and judgment, for the promotion of true religion and the best interests of humanity.

A few weeks before his death, Miss More received from him a short and hurried note, begging her intercession at the throne of mercy for divine aid on a difficult duty which devolved upon him: "My great hope and resource is, what I have always had recourse to in such cases, prayer; give me then your frequent and fervent prayers, and I shall hope for that most powerful protection of a gracious Providence, which I am convinced has never failed in similar cases." The nature of the duty he did not disclose, but on the third day she received the assurance that prayer had had its usual effect, and all was well.

A report having reached the worthy prelate of the formation of a Sunday club under the patronage of the Prince of Wales, this public desecration of holy time filled him with sorrow and alarm. Rallying his wasted strength, he sought the prince, and in solemn language warned him of the fatal influence of his example upon the religion and morals of his kingdom. The prince heard and yielded, and the servant of God departed in peace: a few more days, and he entered upon a Sabbath of eternal rest. Miss More erected a cenotaph to his memory on her grounds at Barley Wood, bearing the inscription:

TO

BEILBY PORTEUS,

LATE LORD BISHOP OF LONDON,

IN GRATEFUL MEMORY OF LONG AND FAITHFUL FRIENDSHIP.

H. M.

CHAPTER XIV.

FALLING LEAVES.

IN the summer of 1810, we find Miss More making a tour among good and agreeable friends in Gloucester, reviving the friendships of earlier days, and adding new ones to the already extended list.

"I have been visiting," she writes to Mrs. Kennicott, "the scenes where we used to gipsy, and traced many a spot where I had picked dry sticks to boil the tea-kettle under a shady oak, or broiled a mutton-chop on knitting-needles. The companions of our harmless rambles are all gone."

Mrs. Montagu, sprightly and beautiful even at fourscore, had died, and a volume of her letters was before the public. Her friend and intimate, Elizabeth Carter, lived a year or two longer, surrounded by all that could make long life venerable and attractive, "honor, love, obedience, and troops of friends."

Miss More was threescore, and if there be an abatement of bodily vigor, there is no slackness of the hidden fires that glow within.

In spite of "tormenting bile," a burdensome correspondence, and almost incessant company, time and strength were not wanting to write "Practical Piety," one of her favorite works in this country, and one which is far superior to many works of a kindred character that have superseded it. After describing what Christianity is as an internal principle, she thus unfolds its practical influence:

"The love of God, as it is the only source of every right feeling and action, so it is the only principle which necessarily involves the love of our fellow-creatures. There is a love of partiality, but not of benevolence; of sensibility, but not of philanthropy; of friends and favorites, of parties and societies, but not of men collectively. It is true, we may and do, without this principle, relieve man's distresses, but we do not bear with his faults. We may promote his fortune, but we do not forgive his offences; above all, we are not anxious for his immortal interests. We could not see him want without pain, but we can see him sin without emotion. We could not hear of a beggar perishing at our door without horror, but we can without concern witness an acquaintance dying without repentance. Is it not strange that we must participate something of the divine nature before we can really love the human? It seems to be an insensibility to sin, rather than want of benevolence to mankind, that makes us naturally pity their temporal and be careless of their spiritual wants: but does not this very insensibility proceed from a want of love to God?"

This discriminating extract is followed by a clear analysis of what is sometimes called "sentimental benevolence," and an estimate of what it is really worth.

"It really feels for the disorders which afflict humanity, at least while it lasts; it really desires to relieve them, and sets about reforming some of the external and more prominent evils, in the hope that if they are cured, those of lesser note will naturally flat away, and society in the end will be righted. Sin is regarded as accidental, rather than radical—an *excuse*, rather than a *cause;* poverty a penalty for wealth, rather than a consequence of idleness and unthrift; restraint, discipline, and punishment, the inexorable decrees of the few, instead of the necessary safeguards for the many; reformation of institutions is more aimed at than regeneration of principles. But it is found to be a far more difficult and perplexing work than was counted for: it is like stopping the leaks of an old building with sand; it gets soon discouraged at the hopeless nature of its task; yet, unwilling to abandon it, still anxious to seem to do even when it knows not what to do or where to begin, it runs to find fault with those who continue patiently laboring, because so much still remains to be done, and rail at their instruments without offering them better. The truth is, this philanthropy springs from the natural sensibilities and sympathies of the heart, which are amiable rather than efficient, self-loving rather than self-sacrificing, the parent of feeling more than of principle, partaking more of the demagogue than the true patriot.

"The disordered state of the world, it must be confessed, is painful and perplexing in the extreme; but the disease lies at the heart and in the core of society, and there is no love for man but that which springs from love to God, which is strong and faithful enough to work for his salvation. The maxims, motives, and aims which control man are wrong, and nothing but the reception of those principles which God has given in the gospel of his Son can essentially improve his inward or better his outward condition. While much, very much may be done to benefit and reform the institutions of society, evils still remain which admit of no cure, but which must be patiently borne; and it is surely far more difficult to bear each other's burden, than to comfort with the promise of removing them. In attempting then to do any permanent good to our fellows, we must not only relieve their distresses, but amend their principles; not only promote their temporal welfare, but be careful for their immortal interests; not only excite their activity, but teach them submission; not only give them alms, but forgive their offences. To do this, you must be patient and painstaking, continuing on, yet ever forbearing. You must lay your account with ingratitude and improvidence, disappointment and reproach. You must meet evils with manliness, and exigencies without fear or disheartening. You are to expend no unavailing sympathy, to utter no useless complaints, to offer no affected condolence, to make no false promises. Your duty is to *labor and to wait.* In order to do this, you must love your fellow-men because Christ loves them; suffer for them because he suffered for them; labor for them because he died for them."

"Practical Piety" cannot be too highly recommended; it is a book for our serious and thoughtful moments, when we desire to inquire calmly and seek sincerely after that obedience which is "perfect and entire, wanting nothing." Its *expression* differs from religious works of a later growth; it contains no fervid appeals, no exaggerated estimates, no startling phrases; it discourses earnestly of our duties and dangers as professed servants of God; it deals candidly and plainly, telling us what we are and what we must be; it shows that no superficial obedience can stand in place of an entire surrender of the whole man to the service of God; it allows no partial standard, or low estimate, or sluggish action in the Christian life.

"Many are reformed," it tells us, "on human motives; many are only partially reformed: but those only who, as our great poet says, are '*reformed altogether*,' are *converted.* There is no complete reformation of the conduct effected without a revolution in the heart. Ceasing from some sins, retaining others in a less degree, or adopting such as are merely creditable, or flying from one sin to another, or ceasing from the external act without any internal change of disposition, is not Christian reformation. The natural bias must be changed. The actual offence will no more be pardoned than cured, if the inward corruption be not eradicated. To be 'alive unto God, through Jesus Christ,' must follow 'death unto sin.' There cannot be new aims and ends where there is not a new principle to produce them."

"It is not casting a set of opinions into a mould and a set of duties into a system, which constitutes the Christian religion. The circumference must have a centre, the body must have a soul, the performances must have a principle. Outward observances were wisely constituted to rouse our forgetfulness, to awaken our secular spirits, to call back our negligent hearts. They were designed to execute holy thoughts, to quicken us to holy deeds, but not to be used as equivalents to either.

"Nothing short of a uniform and stable principle, that fixedness in religion which directs a man in all his actions, aims, and pursuits, to *God as his ultimate end*, can give consistency to his character or tranquillity to his soul."

In speaking of the importance of correcting small faults and cherishing the minor virtues, these making up the sum of human character, it says, "The reason why what are called religious people often differ so little from others in small trials is, that instead of bringing religion to their aid in their lesser vexations, they either leave the disturbance to prey upon their minds, or apply to false reliefs for its removal. Those who are rendered unhappy by frivolous troubles, seek comfort in frivolous enjoyments. But we should apply the same remedy to ordinary trials as to great ones; for as small disquietudes spring from the same cause as great ones, namely, the uncertain and imperfect condition of human nature, so they require the same remedy. You would apply to religion on the loss of your child; apply to it on the loss of your temper. As no calamity is too great for the power of piety to mitigate, so none is too small to experience its beneficial results. Our behavior under the ordinary accidents of life forms a characteristic distinction between different classes of Christians: the least advanced resort to religion on great occasions; the deeper proficient resorts to it on all.

"An acquaintance with the nature of human evils and of their remedy, would check that spirit of complaint which so much abounds, and which often makes so little difference between those who profess religion and those who do not.

"If our duties are not great, they become important by the constant demand that is made for them. They have been called the 'small coin of human life,' and on their perpetual and unobstructed circulation depends much of the comfort and convenience of life. How few of us are called to carry the gospel into distant lands; but which of us is not called every day to adorn its doctrines by gentleness, kindness, and forbearance?"

The excessive strictness of Practical Piety was made a matter of complaint among some of her religious friends.

"The gospel is strict," was her reply; "the cutting off a right hand, or the plucking out of a right eye, though only used as metaphors and illustrations, is surely more strict than any thing I have said. The standard of religion should be always kept high: the very best of us are always sure to pull it down a good many pegs in our practice; but how much lower is the practice of those who fix a lower standard than the New Testament holds out?"

But cannot you write of Christianity in more general terms, like Addison and Johnson, and not dwell so much on the peculiar doctrines of the Bible? they said again.

"Much as I honor and love these," answered she, "their writings would have done a far wider and deeper good, had they not generalized religion so much. The soundness of Johnson's principles is incontestable; but he scarcely ever enters on any evangelical truth. Addison had a devout spirit; still he appears not to have entered into those deep views of evangelical truth which abound in Pascal and Taylor, in Leighton and Hall; and my regret is, that they did not dwell more on the *doctrines* of Christianity, and upon what distinguishes it from all religious systems as a *scheme of salvation.*"

"Compare the influence of Johnson and Addison as moralists and Christians, celebrated and world-read as they are, with Baxter and Doddridge; how do they sink into comparative insignificance before the pungent, searching, humbling teachings of believing men, who took the Bible as God gave it, daring neither to lessen nor to narrow its solemn and awful truths, as they stand recorded on its inspired pages. It is such men only who can meet the wants of sinful man; it is only such preaching and such teaching that can measure the depth of human frailty and corruption, and which can propose a remedy to satisfy the conscious need of the burdened spirit. Men are frail and imperfect and sorrowful; but they are something more, they are *sinners*, and are conscious of a weight of ill-desert of which no one can relieve them. Christian generalities may arrest the ear and please the reason, but they do not and they *cannot* strike the conscience, compel a man to stop, let go his hold on the world, and cry out with an earnestness never felt before, 'What shall I do to be saved?'

"It is only the distinguishing doctrines of the Bible, urged by those who have felt their power, that can have any direct or permanent influence upon the life and conscience of others. Any system short of a recognition of a man's apostasy, his pardon and restoration through Jesus Christ, with the consequent fruits of a holy life, all the tremendous issues of which hang upon immediate action—any system short of this, may it not be repeated, is inoperative and inefficient towards bringing men to repentance and faith, to holiness and heaven. Believers there are all over the church of Christ on earth, who, under God, bless Doddridge and Baxter for the joy set before them; while saints, singing the song of Moses and the Lamb, will be crowns of their rejoicing in the great day."

It was this solemn persuasion of the essential features of Bible truth which gave such power to the teaching and example of Hannah More—a power which offended some, but benefited more. In all her writings, and in all her plans for human good, her great and especial design was to *seek and to save those who are lost*. This was her heart's desire, and it was this which quickened her in her long and wearisome journeys among the neighboring parishes even after the infirmities of age and sickness crept over the body, and gave vigor to her pen while the hand that held it was cramped with pain and benumbed by weakness.

The earnest and heartfelt piety which springs from a believing reception of divine truth is often confounded with gloom and austerity, and yet there is none which can give such cheerfulness to life, and such hope in death. To one who asked whether her serious pursuits had not destroyed her relish for pleasantry, she replied, "As you cannot see those who live with me, you must take my testimony that I am neither a bigot nor a misanthrope; my spirits are good, and even gay. I hope it is no infringement on better things to say, that my bite for humor and a sort of sensible nonsense, is not a whit diminished. A life of ill-health has no ways impaired my constitutional cheerfulness, and I am sometimes afraid that I take more than my share of society."

Practical Piety was followed by Christian Morals, which soon passed through eleven editions.

But while her pen was more busy and instructive than ever, the sisters were compelled to curtail their Sabbath labors. The Mendip schools, like good children of a healthy stock, still looked well and thriving; but neither Hannah nor Patty were longer equal to the fatigue of superintending so large a field: three parishes only continued to share their benefactions, Shipham, Nailsea, and Cheddar their last as well as their first love. Here were teachers who had been twenty years in their service, faithful and well-approved. Men and women, husbands and wives, and heads of families, from little children had grown up in the schools, and become worthy citizens and servants of God: many had passed through sickness and tribulation, having obtained a good report through faith, and at last died ripe with Christian hopes. Peace, good order, and industry everywhere prevailed over the once abandoned district; friendly neighborhoods and happy families, thankful hearts and tidy hearths bore witness that the word of God is valuable for the life that now is, and for that which is to come.

But there is sorrow in Barley Wood: they who have comforted others, themselves need comfort. Mary is not. During five days of suffering, no murmur or complaint escaped her lips; she talked of "going home," and picked out the poor men who should bear her to her narrow cell. The sisters gathered around her dying bed: it was Sabbath morning when she breathed her last.

"How blessed to die on Easter Sunday," said Hannah, "to descend to the grave when Jesus triumphed over it."

Twenty times a day did they visit her cold remains. "I divide the morning between the contemplation of her serene countenance and my favorite Baxter's Saints' Rest," adds Hannah, her tears stayed, as with the eye of faith she sees the eldest, "not lost, but gone before." This was in April, 1813.

When summer came, a journey, with its change of scene and air, was necessary to recruit the exhausted strength of the two younger sisters. They went into Surrey and Kent, drove through the environs of London, visited Henry Thornton, and passed a day with Wilberforce, the home influences of whose quiet but elegant house spoke peace to many a guest.

"What extensive good has Mr. Wilberforce done among young persons of fashion, by the intellectual and religious intercourse of his family!" Miss Hannah exclaims. It was not only in his public acts that Wilberforce was a Christian; in the bosom of his family, in his intercourse with his children, in the frank and chastened courtesy of his manners, his daily life commended the faith which he loved.

"A few such hours," said she, "where inquiring minds know that they shall meet with good company, in the best sense of the word, would, I am sure, fortify the minds and cheer the spirits, as well as confirm the principles of many. I know that many have been deterred from the society of religious persons by some want of discretion and delicacy, which they have been glad to magnify, in order to get quite out of the connection: I am, however, aware that all one's prudence is not sufficient to clear away the charge of enthusiasm which the world is ever watching for an occasion to bring forward against those who exhibit a more than ordinary degree of strictness; but this they must be contented to bear for their *great Master*, who bore so much for them."

But a great improvement was already visible in the higher class of English society. "Twenty years ago," said Jane Porter, "while a child, I have cried to hear people at the table scoff so at religion, with nobody daring to defend it: now such a thing would not be tolerated."

An increasing seriousness and respect for religious things were everywhere manifest; the Sabbath was more strictly observed: levity upon sacred truths was not only regarded vulgar and undignified, but frowned upon. A higher and better tone of moral feeling pervaded the public prints, and the tendency among all classes seemed to be upward. No small part of this change may be traced to the influence of Hannah More, whose literary fame preceded and opened the way for her religious writings. Known and admired in the most elegant and learned circles of the metropolis, it happily became the fashion to read her productions; and thus her works had an entrance and an unconscious influence in circles otherwise adverse to religious reading of so decided a character, and indeed to religious reading of any kind. Nor did fashion here show its usual fickleness: Miss More continued to be read and reread, published and circulated, with an ever-increasing interest and improvement; nor can we ever imagine the time to be, when the Shepherd of Salisbury Plain shall not be reckoned among the most beautiful and touching illustrations of the power of divine grace.

She left the mansion of Wilberforce, and took her way to Strawberry Hill, now the residence of Lady Waldegrave, where a thousand recollections of the past, partly pleasing, but more painful, filled her heart. Here too was Hampton, where for thirty years she passed a portion of every winter with Mrs. Garrick. It had now been several years since they met. Of the old circle who first welcomed her to London, Mrs. Garrick alone was living, and she was past ninety. Miss More hastened to see her: she was absent; but the library, the lawn, the temple of Shakspeare—she would see all for the last time!

"What wit, what talents, what vivacity, what friendship have I enjoyed in this place," she said. "Where are they now? I have been mercifully spared to see the vanity and emptiness of every thing that is not connected with eternity; and seeing this, how heavy will my condemnation be, if I do not lay it to heart."

Her frame is feeble, her step is tottering, her face wrinkled with age; but within, what a fountain of life! What spiritual excellency, what strength, vigor, and serenity, what power in that sinking and sickly frame!

The travellers returned to Barley Wood, and in the autumn Mr. Wilberforce, with his wife and daughters, spent a few delightful days at this "favored seat of intellectual and religious sunshine," as it was afterwards called by one of the sons of this favored guest. A new source of interest and activity opened to the sisters in the formation of a Branch Bible Society in the parish of Wrington. The great difficulty in obtaining any thing like an adequate supply of Bibles for either home or foreign circulation, led to the foundation of the British and Foreign Bible Society as early as 1803, in which all religious parties united alike, without regard to party or sect. No society ever had a broader or more blessed mission; its operations were confined to no creed or country: its field was the world. When a few used to meet in Mr. Hardcastle's counting-room, to consult together and prepare measures for its formation, Wilberforce came also. It was planted a very little seed; it grew up, and has become a goodly tree, yielding her fruit every month, and the leaves of the tree are for the healing of the nations.

The first anniversary of the Wrington Branch was held on the grounds of Barley Wood; the spiritual climate being cold, none of the Mendip gentry opened their mansions. The meeting took place in the wagon-yard; one hundred sat down to dinner, and it being a fine day, the rest dined under the trees.

"Some may think it would have been better to add £20 to our subscription," said Miss More to Wilberforce, "and save ourselves so much trouble; but we take this trouble from a conviction of the contrary. The many young persons of fortune present, by assisting in this little festivity, will learn to connect the idea of innocent cheerfulness with that of religious societies, and may go and do likewise. For no other cause on earth would we encounter so much fatigue." They all enjoyed themselves exceedingly, and the lawn had all the gayety of a public garden.

Let us hear how Barley Wood and its mistress strike a stranger from the West. A lady from Massachusetts pays her a visit. "How did she look?" and "What did Hannah More say?" are fair questions enough.

"Miss More was about seventy-five years old at the time I saw her, with an eye as brilliant as a girl of eighteen, a dark hazel color, with a full, matronly form of medium height. Her dress was of black cambric, with a plain, double muslin handkerchief over it, and a full-ruffled muslin cap. But her conversation, *that* was the charm—interspersed frequently with quotations from Scripture. When we commended her works, and told her we thought great good had been done by them in America, her reply was, 'Oh, if *any* good has been done by them, if the few tinsel talents I possess *may* have been made useful! The Lord is sometimes pleased to employ the feeblest instruments in his service: do not *praise me*, but give God the glory, it is *all* of *him!* You are very encouraging, and I need encouragement.'

"Miss More said 'we might think it an odd speech she was about to make, but that we'—the clergyman and his wife who accompanied me—'could scarcely have found a day in many years, when they were situated as they were to-day. The Bristol Fair is now held, but we do not approve of fairs, and never allow our servants to go; Bonaparte's carriage, however, has been a matter of great curiosity in this family, and one of my sisters has gone with four of our servants—for we dare not trust them alone—to gratify their innocent, though ridiculous curiosity, and you must receive it as a particular mark of friendship'—at the same time taking Mrs. T——'s hand—'if we ask you to take a bit of boiled beef with us; but we must wait on ourselves, and if, under such circumstances, you will partake with us, we shall be happy to have you.'

"On our fearing that to *dine* with them would detain us too long, she kindly said we must take some refreshment. She gave us cold mutton sliced, with bread and butter and beer, all excellent. In the time it was preparing, we went over her cottage, which is neatly elegant, having a beautiful verandah in front, ornamented with a variety of flowers, and rose-trees in bloom, rising even to the *thatched* roof which covers this interesting dwelling. She showed us into a 'chamber for a friend,' commanding a prospect of the whole of Wrington valley, in which are situated twelve parish churches, and which was the birthplace of John Locke, to whose memory she has a monument in her garden. Further west may be seen two islands in the sea, about nine miles from the shore, and she observed that 'their nearest market-town in the same direction is Boston; so,' said she, 'when you reach home, look eastward, and think of me.'

"Miss More told us the place was much endeared to them, from the circumstance of their having planted every tree and shrub, and even laid the first stone for building their cottage, about thirteen years before, with their own hands.

"She took us to her bedroom, which is also a library, and pointed out the excellences of almost every author as we passed them, as familiarly as a parent could the different traits of her children. Baxter and Saurin were her favorite authors. She admired the sublime words of Baxter on his death-bed: when asked by a friend how he was, he replied, opening his eyes, 'Almost well!' meaning he should soon be with Christ in heaven.

"Miss More was not well enough to walk with us over her grounds, but on our return to the house we enjoyed her delightful discourse a little longer in the drawing-room.

"She said much of the evils of hoarding up wealth, and mentioned the death of a friend the previous week by the name of Renolds, who gave away his immense property, restricting himself to bare necessaries.

"'Indeed,' said she, 'an avaricious professor of religion is an anomaly that I cannot understand.'

"Mr. T—— said it was a subject on which he should preach from his own pulpit, when he returned home.

"'Do,' said Miss More, 'and take for your text, But thou, O man of God, flee these things, Tim. 4:11, and think of me.'

"Miss More mentioned 'good news from India'—that a bishop had written that he was then on the sea, going to another part of his diocese, which was five thousand miles in extent, and that a Brahmin of high caste was lately converted entirely by his own study of the Scriptures—'and yet it is said,' she remarked, 'this alone is of no use'—and that he, with more than two hundred of his caste, were soon to be baptized, when he intended coming to Europe, to a university.

"Her sister remarked that 'the evening before, Lord Tinmouth and the Bishop of Gloucester had visited them, and that they had sat conversing until three o'clock in the morning, and all the time the words went as rapidly from one to the other as the bird of a battledoor.'"

Can we not almost see the lady of the manor in her black cambric dress, and full ruffled cap?

Meanwhile Miss More was ready to issue another work, an essay on the Life and Writings of St. Paul—the first edition of which is sold the first day, and she has not a single copy to present to her sisters. It is a true and beautiful portrait of this eminent apostle, whose writings she had studied with profound interest.

Three years had scarcely passed since the first breach in the family circle, when Elizabeth, or Betty as she was familiarly called, followed Mary to the final rest.

Her loss was a serious one to the family at Barley Wood: no one who understands how many wheels there are within a wheel, which need to be kept in harmonious action for a well-regulated household, could undervalue the importance of her position. Beyond her home a large circle also mourned her loss.

The year 1816 and thereabouts witnessed scarcity, depression, and murmuring among the English people. War had burdened the treasury and crippled the resources of the nation; nor could the proclamation of peace immediately restore that prosperity and well-ordered industry which are among her chief blessings. Discontent began everywhere to prevail; hungry men cried out for reform; secret assemblies were holden; unpopular ministers were insulted; pikes were manufactured; and worse than all, the agitation and violence of the times were increased by the circulation of a fresh batch of infidel writings, adding fuel to the flame. The London committees are again in motion: measures must be taken to circulate throughout the veins and arteries of society pure blood, or the whole would be corrupted. Among the publications of the day, Miss More's tracts and songs again play a distinguished part. "Will Chip" reäppeared upon the stage; "Village Disputants," the title having been slightly altered, rapidly ran through ten editions. Her quiet insight of what was necessary, her true woman's tact, which serves the sex so well, enabling them to reach just conclusions without troublesome arguments, caused a fresh demand upon her pen.

"I did not think of turning ballad-monger in my old age," she says, "but the strong and urgent representations which I have had from the highest quarters of the alarming temper of the times, and the spirit of revolution which shows itself more or less in all the manufacturing towns, led me to undertake as a duty a task I would gladly have avoided."

She set herself to work, and in a few weeks wrote a dozen penny and half-penny articles, thousands and tens of thousands of which were circulated far and wide.

"I fear the antidotes are not strong enough to expel the deeply-rooted poison," she says, "but each must do what he can."

"These are awful times, and this tempestuous weather, by putting a stop to the sowing of corn, I fear is preparing for us another season of scarcity. But the Lord God omnipotent reigneth; what consolation to be assured of this!"

Miss More wrote and published and republished many of her former tracts and stories suited to the present exigencies, while her heart was aching over the slow and sure decay of her sister Sally, whose sprightliness and wit still enchanted her friends. For months she knew there was no prospect of recovery, neither could any thing materially alleviate her disease. Her sufferings were sometimes intense, which drew forth the frequent exclamation, "Poor Sally, you are in dreadful pain." "I am indeed, but it is well," was her calm reply. Indeed, so playful still was her conversation, so quiet and patient her temper, it was hard to believe her dying.

While yet able to stay in the family sitting-room, and employ herself a little with her work-basket, she gave up her old seat at the bow-window, lest the beauties of the earthly scene might draw her away from the frequent contemplation of the heavenly. At last, no longer able to bear a sitting posture, she was assisted up stairs—for the last time, she well knew. Before leaving, she looked back, and cast a parting glance about the room: it was a silent and solemn farewell; no word was spoken. Her sufferings rapidly increased. Unable to hear any connected reading, Hannah and Patty repeated detached verses from the Bible, in which she often joined. Once, having lain long insensible, a favorite text was recited. "Can any thing be finer than that? It makes one's face shine," she suddenly exclaimed.

When life seemed nearly gone, her physician took her by the hand, and bade her good morning. Lifting her hands in holy transport, she said, "Oh for the glorious morning of the resurrection! but there are some gray clouds between."

"Oh the blood of Christ! He died for me. God was man. Talk of the cross, the precious cross, the King of love!"

"Four months," writes Hannah to Mrs. Kennicott, "we have watched over her increasing disease. Poor Patty and I watched over this bed of suffering, but our distress was mingled with much consolation. I cannot do justice to her humility, her patience, her submission. It was sometimes more than resignation; it was a spiritual triumph over the suffering of her tormented body. She often said, 'I have never prayed for recovery, but pardon. I do not fear death, but sin.'

"My three sisters have quitted the world in the same order of succession as they entered it. My turn, in course, would be next. Pray for me, that I may *do* and *suffer* the whole will of God."

A friend who visited Barley Wood after the last sad bereavement, writes thus of the remaining two sisters: "Feeling as they do very deeply the sad breach made in their circle, they are wisely, cheerfully, and piously submissive to this appointment of Providence; and neither their talents nor their vivacity are in the least subdued. I am disposed to believe that they will be blessed to the last with the retention of those faculties which they have employed so well. With Patty I had a long and interesting conversation. This interesting woman is suffering with exemplary patience the greatest pain: not a murmur escapes her, though at night especially groans and cries are inevitably extorted, and the moment after the paroxysm she is ready to resume with full interest and animation whatever may have been the subject of conversation. Hannah is still herself. She took the Rev. Charles Forster and me to drive to Brockley Combe; in the course of which her anecdotes, her wit, her powers of criticism, and her admirable talent at recitation, had ample scope."

How serene and beautiful is the picture! We forget that old age and sickness are there, so repulsive to youth, so uninteresting and unattractive to busy, bustling middle life. Hannah is seventy-three, and Patty an invalid; therefore when Sally died, who cared for the flowers, "The garden will be neglected; there is no one left to do like Sally." Ah, no; Hannah went out to meet the spring flowers: she gathered the roses and bound up the honeysuckles, and the garden bloomed as sweetly as it used to.

CHAPTER XV.

A GOLDEN HARVEST.

Miss More sits at her desk correcting the fifteenth edition of Cœlebs, and the eleventh of Practical Piety. She speaks thus: "In spite of the dull task of reforming points and particles, I found the revisal of the last especially a salutary and mortifying employment. How easy it is to be good upon paper! I felt myself humbled, even to a sense of hypocrisy, to observe—for I had forgotten the book—how very far short I had fallen of the habits and principles and interior sanctity which I had found it so easy to recommend to others. I hardly read a page which did not carry some reproach to my own heart. I frequently think of a line which Prior puts into the mouth of Solomon,

"'They brought my Proverbs to confute my life.'

"Cœlebs in Search of a Wife" had now been before the public ten years, with a rapid sale both in England and the United States. "Never was more pain bound up in two volumes," she said, alluding to her illness while writing it.

Dr. Henderson, the entertaining tourist of Iceland, found Cœlebs enlivening the long evenings of many a circle in that ice-bound region; Swedish youths learned from it lessons of wisdom; it was translated into French and German; and may it not be hoped that young men and maidens, and the newly married, became wiser and better for having read it?

Nor was Russia impenetrable to her influence. The "Shepherd of Salisbury Plain," with "Charles the Footman," and several of their excellent companions, made an extensive circuit throughout that empire; and she received the assurance from a pious Russian princess, that they were opening the way for other works of a kindred character.

India also reaped the benefit of her labors. Portions of "Moses in the Bulrushes" were presented to Miss More, written in Cingalese on the palmyra leaf, and many of her writings were translated both in Tamul and Cingalese. Sir Alexander Johnstone, Chief-Justice of Ceylon, on his return to England, visited Barley Wood to assure her of the interest which they excited among the natives, and to bespeak a poem from her gifted pen, to be sung on the anniversary of the abolition of domestic slavery on that island. Servitude existed among the Dutch settlers of Ceylon when it fell into the hands of the English, who at the time guaranteed to all the inhabitants their rights of private property; nor were they willing to relinquish this among the rest, until Sir Alexander having secured to them some important privileges from the English government, in gratitude to him they resolved that all children born of their slaves after the 12th of August, 1816, should become free. Miss More wrote a little dramatic poem, called the "Feast of Freedom," which was translated into the native language by two young priests then receiving an English education under the care of Dr. Adam Clarke, and became a great favorite in Ceylon.

"What a pleasure must it afford you, my dear madam," wrote the Chief-Justice to the author, "to have the power of producing such moral improvement by your writings, not only throughout Europe, but throughout Asia also; for I am convinced that your writings have had a greater effect, and have been more generally read, than any other works which have been written for the last hundred years."

The next pilgrims to Barley Wood, Miss More says, "are two very interesting and sensible Persians, who have been studying the literature, arts, and sciences of this country, and are returning home with great acquisitions of knowledge. I never saw any Asiatics before who had energy, spirit, and curiosity: these are all alive. In my garden is an urn to the memory of Locke, who was born in our village. When they saw it, they exclaimed in rapture, 'What, Locke the metaphysician?' They go to our different places of worship, attend Bible and other public meetings, and seem to have fewer prejudices against Christianity than you would suppose. They particularly admire Job and Isaiah, and those parts of the Old Testament which have the most orientalism. Their figures and costume are striking, their manners very genteel. I was amused to see the Mohammedans drink a little wine. The most literary of the two wished to have something of mine as a memento. I gave him Practical Piety, which he said he would translate when he got home."

The formation and growth of the religious

institutions which have so distinctly marked the beginning of the present century, were a source of unspeakable gratitude to Hannah More; and "I sometimes regret, foolishly enough," she said, "that some of my earliest and dearest friends did not live to promote and rejoice in the wonderful prosperity of such as each particularly delighted in. Dean Tucker, Dr. Kennicott, and Bishop Horne would have been among the most zealous supporters of the conversion of the Jews, as Dr. Johnson would of the slave abolition and the Bible and missionary societies. Bishop Porteus would have rejoiced in the prosperity of all. To descend to so poor a thing as myself and my writings, the gratification I feel in that measure of success which it has pleased God to grant unworthy me, when so many abler and better persons have been neglected, is much diminished by the loss of the above-named and many others, who would have taken a warmer interest in what concerned me than I deserved, and that from partial kindness. But all this is necessary, salutary, and right."

In the spring of 1818, both sisters were so much shattered by sickness, that friends suspended their accustomed visits to Barley Wood, and left the invalids to that undisturbed repose which they greatly needed. Its benefits upon Hannah were soon apparent; both mind and body were improved, and she, under that abiding sense of "doing with her might," began and prepared a small work, called "Moral Sketches of Prevailing Opinions and Manners, Foreign and Domestic," to which were added her "Reflections on Prayer," so deservedly known in this country.

The first edition sold on the first day, and realized fifteen thousand dollars.

In spite of the great popularity and excellent tendency of her writings, Miss More seems ever to have made a low estimate of her merits, declaring on one occasion, that "the only remarkable thing which belonged to her as an author was, that she had written eleven books after the age of sixty."

The attachment of the two surviving sisters was most tender and true; they had lived much together; their Sunday labors had been equally shared; they loved the same things, and in company had visited often and again the same places; the "sweet sense of kindred" had been strengthened by the hallowed associations of a long and endeared partnership in every good word and work; and now they two were all that were left of the happy band that once sported on old Stapleton Green.

As months and years passed by, each was admonished that frail was her hold on life, and each sought to live in preparation for the last summons. Miss Patty wrote in her account-book, "This is the last I shall ever want;" and every scrap of paper in her desk bore record of a willing and waiting spirit: yet "she is eyes and hands and feet" to Hannah, who might well exclaim, "How *can* I give thee up?"

The Wilberforces made a short sojourn at Barley Wood in the early part of September, 1819. On the last day of their visit, Patty accompanied them to dear old Cheddar, Brockley Combe, and among the green winding ways of the region, and then remained up long after her usual time, talking over Hannah's first introduction to London, with all her wonted animation. It was late when she came to her sister's bedside to say good-night. "Our Wilberforce and I have had such a nice hour's chat," said she cheerfully. A few hours later, and she awoke in the pangs of death. "Oh, I love my sufferings," she exclaimed; "they come from God, and I love every thing which comes from him."

Whenever the mind wandered, the ruling passion, strong in death, issued its orders like these: "Be sure let that old woman have her shoes;" "Do not forget the old man's clothes;" intent still upon those objects which had formed her chief interest and daily business of many years.

"I have lost," said the stricken survivor, "my chief earthly comfort, companion, counsellor, and fellow-laborer. I need not tell you that my grief is exquisite. God doubtless saw that I leaned too much on this weak prop, and therefore in mercy withdrew it, that I might depend more exclusively on himself. When I consider how infinitely greater *her gain* is than *my loss*, I am ashamed of my weakness. I can truly say, however, that it has not been mixed with one murmuring thought—I kiss the rod and adore the hand that employs it. I do not so much brood over my loss as over the many mercies which accompany it. I bless God that she was spared to me so long; that her last trial, though sharp, was short; that she is spared feeling *for me* what I now feel *for her;* and though I must finish my journey alone, yet it is a very short portion of my pilgrimage which remains to be accomplished."

"In our numerous charity schools she had exerted herself for thirty-two years with the most unwearied perseverance," wrote Miss More, "and I may be allowed to add—now she is gone—with great success in training up numbers of useful members of the community, and many souls for heaven. Never was any private individual more lamented. Our poor gardener said 'she had made as many garments for the poor as Dorcas, and had as many tears shed over her death-bed.' Several funeral sermons were preached for her in the neighborhood, and our neighbors have put on mourning."

Almost every day used to come messages or applications to Barley Wood, from the poor or sick or needy of the surrounding parishes, in request of relief and sympathy, found always within its friendly gates. For several weeks after Miss Patty's death, no one of them knocked at the door, or came near the house. At last the schoolmaster of Shipham with his donkey and panniers came to receive his stated supply of books for the schools. "It is very long since we have seen any of you," said Miss

Hannah. "Why, madam, they be so cut up, they have not the heart to come," answered the old man mournfully.

Letters of sympathy, affection, and condolence came in upon the mourner from all quarters, and friends flocked around to relieve by their kind offices that void which none could again fill.

"Many people under a similar affliction are apt to say that it is of too deep a nature to admit of consolation from the sympathy of friends. I am not of their opinion," said this honored disciple; "I feel the sympathy of kind and Christian friends very soothing to my mind, and I bless God for affording me, in his mercy and goodness, such a source of comfort."

The withered branch will not long survive: so thought and feared the friends who waited and watched around her. During the spring and summer of 1820, she seemed gradually wasting beneath the repeated and violent seizures of her old complaint: speaking of her burning fever, "Nothing but the last icy hand will cool me," said she. "Poor Patty, I shall soon join her. I hope I shall feel the same patience and submission as dear Patty did. I have great comfort and quietness in my mind."

"I have never known," she said to a clerical friend, "much of those triumphs which I hear of, but I have never been destitute of consolation, trust, and reliance—not that unauthorized calmness which some deem to be always a symptom of peace to the soul."

"You have been a blessing to the world," spoke one near her.

"No, mine has been but a poor little way: I *have* done nothing, I *could* do nothing. The righteousness, mercies, and merits of Christ are all in all."

"How long, O Lord, how long?" she exclaimed, in the extremity of her suffering.

"If you need all this, madam," said one of her attendants, "we may be well filled with dismay."

"The blood of Christ is sufficient: there is no acceptance for the best without it, and with it the worst need not fear obtaining pardon and salvation upon repentance; but it must be profound *heart-repentance*."

Months of suffering passed by, and her resignation in sorrow, her patience in sickness, her forgiveness of injuries, afforded an eloquent commentary upon the holy doctrines which it was the aim of her writings to enforce.

But God was graciously pleased to raise up his aged servant, and restore to her a comfortable measure of health.

In the worst of her illness, Cadell wrote to entreat her to prepare a preface for a new edition of "Moral Sketches," with a short tribute to our lamented king. "My friend wrote him word it was utterly impossible," she related afterwards; "that I might as well attempt to fly as to write. A week after, supposing me to be better, he again renewed his entreaty. I was not better, but worse. I fancied, however, that what was difficult might not be impossible. So having got everybody out of the way, I furnished myself with pen, ink, and paper, which I concealed in my bed, and next morning in a high fever, with my pulse above a hundred, without having formed one thought, bolstered up, I began to scribble. I got on about seven pages, my hand being almost as incompetent as my head. I hid my scrawl and said not a word, while my doctor and my friend wondered at my increased debility. After a strong opiate, I next morning returned to my task of seven pages more, and delivered my almost illegible papers to my friend to transcribe and send away. I got well scolded, but I loved the king, and was carried through by a sort of affectionate impulse; so it stands as a preface to the seventh edition. You will be as much surprised as myself that this slight work should have made its way so rapidly in these distracted times, which the bookseller tells me have been the most unfavorable to literature that he has ever known. The preface is such a meagre performance as you would expect from the writer, and the strange circumstances of the writing."

Neither sickness nor sorrow subdued the wonderful elasticity of her mind, alert to the call of duty, and pressing into service a weak and suffering frame.

Called upon to make some arrangements which anticipated the future, she added, "Not that I have the remotest idea of living through the winter; but we must *plan* for time, and *prepare* for eternity."

"I often think," she said one day, "that we are not thankful enough for negative mercies. I have often felt grateful that I have never been confined in a madhouse, a prison, or a court."

While slowly regaining strength, unable to endure either much company or great fatigue, she relieved the monotony of her confinement by composing "Bible Rhymes," pleasant verses for the young.

"People are too apt, at an advanced age," she remarked, "to imagine, because they were able to do but little, they were exempted from doing any thing; but our work is never finished while we are on earth, and when we have but one talent left, we must strive to the last to make the most of it."

"I can find sufficient employment, which, if not splendid, is not quite useless," she writes to an old friend. "At Bristol, Clifton, and Bath, they have an annual bazaar for the different charitable societies, which, by means of contributions of ladies' different work, produces a good deal of money. You will say that in my old age I am brought so low as to write half-penny papers. Every year I write some such trifle. The ladies who conduct the bazaars in the different places, get these paltry papers printed sometimes on colored papers, and by selling them for a shilling, £20 have been collected in a year. I spend all my leisure in knitting garters and muffatees, a little decorated; these, by the lady-customers giving five times more than they are worth, bring in the year no contemptible sum."

No one perhaps ever set more value on her time than did Hannah More; how else could she have accomplished so much with the various hinderances which sickness and society threw in her way?

"What a large portion of time may be improvidently squandered," she remarks; "what days and nights may be suffered to waste themselves, if not criminally, yet *inconsiderately*—if not loaded with evil, yet *destitute of good;* how much consumed in worthless employments, frivolous amusements, listless indolence, idle reading, and vain imaginations: and one can *never* make a right use of time who turns it over to chance, or who lives without any definite scheme for its employment, or any fixed object for its end."

Upon this subject she again speaks.

"Through the unwearied kindness of more Christian friends than any other unworthy creature was ever blessed with, I see through 'my loophole of retreat,' or rather hear of whatever interesting is going on. My conclusion is, that wickedness is wickeder than it used to be, and that goodness is better. Religion certainly has increased much among the higher classes in England, and perhaps still more in Ireland. Yet I will still venture to say, even to the religious world, 'I have a few things against thee.'

"With no small number of happy exceptions, I cannot help observing the common fault of good people—the *misappropriation of time.* I will only instance two particulars of the evil, of which they do not seem to me to be sufficiently aware—*music and light reading.* Twenty years ago, when I wrote 'Strictures on Female Education,' Bishop Cleaves of St. Asaph was at Bath. He was much attached to me, though we differed on many points. Talking on this subject, he was so much of my opinion, that he wrote the following statement, which I inserted in a note in the first volume: 'Suppose your pupil to begin music at six years of age, and to continue the average of four hours a day at her instrument—a very low calculation—Sundays excepted, till she is eighteen, the statement stands thus: three hundred days multiplied by four, the number of hours amounts to twelve hundred; this multiplied by twelve, which is the number of years, amounts to fourteen thousand four hundred hours!'

"I come now to the *reading.* I pass over

Byron and his compeers in sin and infamy, though I have known some good people who now and then take a slice even of this highly seasoned corruption. I pass over the more loose and amatory novels, and take my stand on what is said to be safe ground, the novels of that unparalleled genius Walter Scott. Now I would not have it supposed that I have not read with delight and admiration all his poetry. This is a repast that might be taken with safety, though certainly not with profit, for it would be difficult to find another specimen of such admirable works with so few maxims for the improvement of life and manners. Let that pass: they gratify the taste without vitiating the imagination; add to this, they were written at reasonably distant periods from each other, so that we were refreshed without being crammed. We come now to his novels, in which his fecundity is as marvellous as his invention. I have read one volume and a half, in which the powers of his vigorous and versatile mind were conspicuous; but from what I have since read in reviews, I rather see the absence of much evil than the presence of much good. I of all people ought not to find fault with authors for writing too much;

yet I must return to my first position, the misapplication of time. Had he written before the flood, when perhaps there were not so many books in the world as he has introduced into it, all would have been well; he would have been a benefactor to the antediluvian Hilpahs and Zylpahs. A life of eight hundred years might be allowed the perusal of the whole of his volumes; a proportionate quantity in each century would have been delightful; but for our poor scanty threescore years and ten, it is too much. Nay, I underestimate the chronology: I believe they have all been produced nearly in odd *ten* years. Now I readily grant, that to the mass of readers the reading of these works should not be prohibited. To the gay, the worldly, and the dissipated, it is perhaps as safe, and even more safe, than any of their other pleasurable resources, being often their only intellectual one. The strong sense, lively exhibition of character, and animated style, certainly afford aliment to the mind. My remarks are limited to a certain class of readers, who have made a strict profession of religion. If indeed our time is to be accounted for as scrupulously as the other talents committed to us, *how will their reckoning stand?* In the case of some, it is almost the only talent they have. Such ought to be especially careful that this one be rightly employed, as we have an awful lesson on the danger of unprofitableness."

On October 22, 1822, Miss More writes to a friend, "I was much affected yesterday with a report of the death of my ancient and valued friend Mrs. Garrick. She was in her hundredth year. I spent above twenty winters under her roof, and gratefully remember, not only their personal kindness, but my first introduction through them into a society remarkable for rank, literature, and talent."

Behold her working for our American Board of Missions.

"A drawing of my little habitation having found its way to New York, they have made a very good engraving of it, which their Board of Foreign Missions is selling; and they are sanguine enough to expect the sale will enable them to build a school in the distant island of Ceylon for poor girls, which they intend doing me the honor of calling Barley Wood." A smile of gratification steals over her countenance.

"I find a good deal of time to work with

my *hands*, while Miss Frowd reads for the entertainment of my *head*," she adds a while after; "and the learned labors of my knitting-needle are now amassing to be sent to America for the Barley Wood school at Ceylon; so you see I am still good for something."

The history of this school is thus: the plan of a girl's school in Ceylon was suggested to a lady in Massachusetts by a letter from the Rev. Mr. Woodward, missionary of the American Board at Ceylon, addressed to the Society of Inquiry at Princeton Theological Seminary, in which he mentioned that associations of ladies might be formed in America to build school-houses for girls, which would cost about thirty dollars, each school bearing the name of the association which supported it.

"I had just then," says the lady, "received a print of Barley Wood from a relation in England; finding it much admired, and many wishing to possess a copy, I united with a friend, who like myself was gratuitously collecting funds for the Board, in the risk of having the print engraved for the benefit of foreign missions. I wrote to Mr. Woodward, with the approbation of Mr. Evarts, that the avails of my part of the engraving were to be appropriated to the building of a bungalow and the support of a girl's school within the limits of his missionary field, requesting him at the same time to select a site as nearly like Barley Wood as could be found, and as early as possible to make the pupils acquainted with the character and works of Hannah More.

"The school was accordingly established in 1823, and the house has been used also as a place of public worship on the Sabbath. I sent copies of the engraving to Mr. Woodward and also to Miss More, who was so much pleased with the plan of a school in memory of her residence, that she immediately sent for its support ten pounds; the next year ten more; the year following twenty, besides bequeathing to it at her death one hundred pounds, which, together with the avails of the engraving, formed a fund for the enlargement and permanent support of the school."

"Barley Wood in Ceylon!" humorously responded an old correspondent, the oldest then living, Sir William Pepys, to whom she communicated the plan. "How this will puzzle some future commentator of your works, who will find some obscure tradition, that for some reason or other—most probably he will say, for the laudable purpose of disseminating religion—our author took this long voyage, and in commemoration of it, gave the name of her own residence to the school, which she evidently established in this island."

Her correspondence at this time was extensive and burdensome. "I see a good deal of company," she tells us, "but the *post* occupies and fatigues me more than my guests. If you saw my table on most days, you would think, were I not a minister of state, I was become at least a clerk in a public office.

"The mass of books and pamphlets which I have from America would surprise you. I do not naturally love republicans; but these people appear really to be making such rapid advances, that they seem to be determined to run with us the race of glory."

Bishop Chase of Ohio paid her a visit in July of 1824, at the anniversary of the Wrington Bible Society, when with a party of seventeen others he dined at Barley Wood, still hospitably open to numerous and admiring guests. The venerable hostess was unable to appear at table, but she received the company in her own apartment after dinner, where a long and animated conversation was kept up for several hours, in which she bore a distinguished part. Her powers of conversation even at seventy-nine were almost unrivalled; so rich, so eloquent, so judicious, so appropriate. "You could not touch her," says one, "without finding her electrical wit, genius, and godliness; her speech was always with wit, seasoned with grace, and ministered to the edifying of the hearers."

Besides the larger appropriations demanded by her schools and the various missionary and charitable objects in which she took a deep interest, her benefactions went into humbler and more retired channels; students were aided in their books and education, young clergymen in purchasing their libraries, and poor widows in eking out their scanty incomes; twenty guineas, a legacy just received from some dignitary whose name she had never heard, were sent to Mrs. Judson for the redemption of two little Burmah slaves; and ten pounds were once sent to Miss Hannah Adams at Boston, on receiving her history of the Jews, and learning that her efforts were made in behalf of a widowed sister and aged father."

On the reception of one hundred pounds

from the son of Sir William Pepys, who had for many years been in the habit of making her an almoner of his bounty, and at whose death his son thus evinced his reverence for his memory, her reply admits us to take, as it were, a parting glance at Cheddar, and a pleasant farewell of the comfort and prosperity which, like the green grass, is creeping around the Mendip Ridge.

"I most thankfully accept the liberal sum you so generously offer. It is indeed most gratuitous on your part, and very acceptable on mine, as my schools consist of six hundred children, and the friends that used to help me out a little are dead. I do not know if I ever mentioned to my admirable correspondent that, attached to my schools, in three different parishes, I instituted thirty-five years ago a female club for the parents of my children. I continue to give them an annual festivity, when every girl bred in my schools and belonging to their respective clubs, if they have maintained a virtuous character, receives what they are pleased to call the bride's portion of the club-pay. This envied portion does not amount to a guinea; but I think it has helped to promote sobriety. I have the satisfaction to know that by petty accumulations and long perseverance, though the members of the club only subscribe sixpence a month, I shall leave these poor people possessed of nearly two thousand pounds in the three parishes. I have long since placed it in the funds, where it is accumulating. I have put it in the trustees' hands. The club is now no further expense to me, except the annual feast, where my valuable companion represents me. Since my inability to be with them, to give it more credit, ten neighboring clergymen, with some other gentry, attend, and make tea for the poor women. I should not have dwelt so long on this subject, but as an instance of what *perseverance and petty saving may accomplish.* It explains how misers with small means grow rich by petty savings."

Life has gone through its spring of hope, its summer work, the autumn harvest; and now, though winter chills are benumbing the limbs, within is glowing a heavenly flame, without, the friendly warmth of human kindness. How sweetly it leans on the unseen arm. "*When* and *whether* belong to Him who governs both worlds. I have nothing to do but to trust. I bless God I enjoy great tranquillity of mind, and am willing to depart and be with Christ when it is his will; but I leave it in his hands, who does all things well," is the language of Hannah More, with eighty years' experience of the goodness and grace of Him in whom she believed.

CHAPTER XVI.

PASSING AWAY.

EVENING shadows were fast creeping around the lengthened days of Hannah More. Her life, prolonged far beyond threescore years and ten, was slowly ebbing amid the fragrant lawns and shady groves of Barley Wood, when a strange and unexpected disclosure in her family history drove her from its bosom, and compelled her to find another home.

Delicate health had almost entirely confined her to her chamber for the last seven years, and necessarily withdrawn her from household occupations; nor could Miss Frowd, her daily friend and companion since Patty's death, be supposed to exercise any very thorough inspection or strong influence over family servants, old in her service, and long used to the ways and wants of their mistress: but Miss More's kindness and confidence were alike disregarded and betrayed. Although trained to the practice of every Christian duty, illustrated by the brightest examples of piety, breathing an atmosphere of purity and love, and pensioners upon her bounty, her servants proved false to their trust, and betrayed the interests of their too indulgent mistress: to fill their pockets, frauds, impositions, and thefts were for years carried on in her kitchen; her charities had been diverted from their appropriate channels; orders sent to traders which were never issued; while their midnight revelries began to be the scandal of the neighborhood. Miss More disregarded for a time the damaging hints concerning her household, until at length they became unmistakably confirmed, and she felt that decided measures must be immediately taken. Two lines of conduct were marked out by her counsellors: one an entire change in the domestic cabinet, and the other a removal from Barley Wood to a situation less cumbered with care. After a short but severe struggle she chose the latter. The Rev. Dr. Whalley offered her his convenient and elegant house in Windsor Terrace, Clifton, and thither she concluded to remove.

"I have been quite overwhelmed by this heavy blow," she writes to Miss Roberts. "I strive and pray fervently for divine support and direction; but such is the variety of difficulties which await me the next month, that I sink under the thought. I bless God that I slept last night, but, like the disciples, it was from sorrow: my kind partner in these sufferings, Miss Frowd, is, I am grieved to say, in bed with a severe cold; this adds much to my distress. You must indeed, my dear friends, you must come and advise me. I would consult you what gentleman I shall get to stay with me in the dreaded moment of separation.

"The shocking conduct of the people below it seems has been long the subject of discourse with the whole neighborhood; I alone was left in ignorance through false kindness. I am more obliged to dear Mr. H—— than I can say; he is a true Christian friend. I really think this shock has hurt my hearing and my memory."

The morning of final leave-taking at length arrived, a cloudy April day. The servants, who, surmising a change, had begun to treat her with personal disrespect, were paid a quarter's wages in advance by their generous and forgiving mistress, and for ever dismissed from her service.

Several gentlemen, with affectionate assiduity, came to support her through her last farewell to Barley Wood—beloved Barley Wood, whose roses and jessamines had for twenty-seven years breathed their fragrance and flung their beauty upon her daily paths—Barley Wood, whose walls and walks were instinct with the treasured memories of the past—Barley Wood, where the sisters dwelt in the mellow light of their declining days, and where, one by one, like ripened sheaves, they had been gathered to the eternal harvest.

Descending the stairs with a placid countenance, she was led into the room below, hung with the portraits of friends long gone, and gazed upon them for a few moments in silence; then hurried with tottering steps towards the carriage. "Ah," she sadly said, "I am driven like Eve from Paradise, but not by angels."

Her elastic and thankful spirit was not slow to discern the beauties of her new home, which commanded a bold and delightful prospect of Leigh woods and Nightingale valley, with the blue Avon winding between. Her face glowed with delight, as her dim eye lingered on the rich expanse.

"I was always," she exclaimed, "delighted with fine scenery, but my sight of late years has been too dim to discern the distant beauties of the vale of Wrington. It has pleased

Providence to ordain me in my last days a view no less beautiful, all the features of which my eye can embrace."

Miss More's ready and gentle acquiescence in this providential ordering of her affairs gratified her friends, and reflected peace and homelikeness throughout her new abode. "Clifton is very pleasant," she gratefully declares; "fewer cares and more comforts." A few months after the settlement, she pleasantly writes to Wilberforce, "I am diminishing my worldly cares. I have sold Barley Wood, and have just parted with the copyright to Cadell of those few of my writings which I had not sold him before. I have exchanged the eight 'pampered minions' for four sober servants. I have greatly lessened my house expenses, which enables me to maintain my schools and enlarge my charities. My schools alone, with clothing and rent, cost me two hundred and fifty pounds a year. Dear good Miss Frowd looks after them, though we are removed much farther from them. The squire of Cheddar attends them for almost the whole of Sunday, and keeps and sends me an accurate statement of merits and wants; so that I have many comforts.

As I have sold my carriage and horses, I want no coachman; as I have no garden, I want no gardener. I have two pious clergymen whom I call my chaplains, and who frequently devote an evening to expound and pray with my family, uniformly on Saturdays. My most kind and skilful physician, Dr. Carrick, who used to have twelve miles to come to me, has now not much above two hundred yards. As to your kind visit, we can give you two beds, and one for a female servant; I am sorry I can do no more. The house, though good, furnishes few conveniences. We have no servants' hall, of course no second table; but we are surrounded with hotels and lodging-houses, etc. It is delightful that we shall meet once more this side of Jordan. Miss Frowd desires her best respects. She is my great earthly treasure. She joins to sincere piety great activity and useful knowledge. She has the entire management of my family, and manages well. She reads well, and reads much to me. I have much more to say, and much, I trust, to hear, when we meet."

But if Clifton released its venerable occupant from home cares, it opened the door to hosts of visitors whose flittings would never have extended to Wrington. Her conversational powers still retained their brilliancy and freshness; her liveliness of manner, chastened by time and sorrow, was blended with a heart-warming Christian love, inspiring both old and young with confidence and affection, while many were attracted towards her by the world-wide reputation of her writings and labors. Nearly four hundred visited her in the first three weeks, which so exhausted her strength and consumed her time, that two days in a week were set apart for general visitors, her "levee days" as they were called; while to her most intimate friends she was at all times accessible.

One day in playful mood she sketched her Court at Windsor Terrace. "The Duke of Gloucester, Sir Thomas Acland, Sir Edmund Hartapp, and Mr. Harford are my sportsmen; Mr. Battersby, Mr. Pigott, and Mrs. Addington my fruiterers; Mrs. Walker Gray my confectioner; Mr. Edward Brice my fishmonger; Dr. Carrick my state physician and zealous friend; Mrs. La Touche my silk mercer and clothier; Bishop of Salisbury my oculist; Misses Roberts my counsellors, *not* solicitors, for they give more than they take; Misses David my old friends and new neighbors; Messrs. Hensman and Elwin my spiritual directors; Mr. Wilberforce my guide, philosopher, and friend; Miss Frowd my domestic chaplain, secretary, and house apothecary, knitter, and lamplighter, missionary to my numerous and learned seminaries, and without controversy, the queen of clubs," in allusion to the village clubs already mentioned; "Mr. Huber my incomparable translator, who by his superiority puts the original out of countenance; Mr. Cadell accoucheur to the muses, who has introduced many a sad sickly brat to see the light, but whispers that they must not depend on a long life."

Barley Wood was sold to William Harford, Esq., and her business interests were so adjusted that no cares were left to harass the infirmities of that period when the grasshopper becomes a burden.

Repeated attacks of inflammatory disease in the region of the chest often brought her extremely low, from which, through the unremitted care and faithful attentions of Miss Frowd, she again and again revived, until November of 1832, when the seizure became more violent, prostrating both the mind and body, and rendering the remaining ten months of her earthly pilgrimage months of extreme weakness, of wakeful nights and restless days, unalleviated by any hope of favorable change, except the heavenly rest. Her pious ejaculations were the utterance of a soul ripening for glory.

"Grow in grace," she earnestly whispered to her attendants, "grow in grace, and in the knowledge of our Lord Jesus Christ;" "Jesus is all in all," "God of grace." "God of light, God of light, whom have I in heaven but thee?" "What can I do—what can I *not* do with Christ? I know that my Redeemer liveth." "Happy, happy are these, who are expecting to meet in a better world. The thought of that world lifts the mind above itself. Oh the love of Christ, the love of Christ!"

Long waiting, "My dear, do people *ever* die?" she said to her friend. "Oh glorious grave! It pleases God to affect me for my good, to make me humble and thankful. Lord, I believe, I *do* believe with all the powers of my weak, sinful heart. Lord Jesus, support me in that trying hour when I most need it. It is a glorious thing to die."

When some one spoke of the good deeds which had adorned her life, she quickly replied, "Talk not so vainly: I utterly cast them from me, and fall low at the foot of the cross."

Thus she waited until the 6th of September, 1833. The usual family devotions were attended at her bedside in the morning; her wasted hands were devoutly raised in prayer, while her countenance glowed with unwonted light; she lay all day quietly and speaking not, while a radiance as from the land of glory illumined her sunken features. In the early night she extended her arms, calling "Patty." A few more hours and she sweetly fell asleep in Jesus, on the dawning of the 7th, in the eighty-ninth year of her age. Five days afterwards Miss More's remains were conveyed to Wrington, and consigned to the family vault by the Rev. Thomas Biddulph, Rector of St. James at Bristol.

All the shops were closed, and the church-bells tolled their solemn requiem, as a long procession followed her to the grave, joined at its arrival at Barley Wood by large numbers of the neighboring gentry, clergy, peasantry and multitudes of little children.

In the village churchyard, beneath a yew and willow, the traveller beholds a plain stone, marking the final resting-place of the five good sisters, and bearing the simple inscription:

"BENEATH ARE DEPOSITED THE MORTAL REMAINS OF FIVE SISTERS:

MARY MORE DIED 18TH OF APRIL, 1813, AGED 75 YEARS.

ELIZABETH MORE DIED 16TH OF JUNE, 1816, AGED 76 YEARS.

SARAH MORE DIED 17TH OF MAY, 1817, AGED 74 YEARS.

MARTHA MORE DIED 16TH OF SEPTEMBER, 1819, AGED 60 YEARS.

HANNAH MORE DIED 7TH OF SEPTEMBER, 1833, AGED 89 YEARS.

ALL THESE DIED IN FAITH,
ACCEPTED IN THE BELOVED.
HEBREWS 11:13. EPHESIANS 1:6."

A handsome fortune had been accumulated by the industry and talent of these ladies; Miss Hannah More having realized from her pen alone, one hundred and fifty thousand dollars. A large portion of it was bequeathed to public institutions, whose fortunes and influences she had long followed with deep and hearty interest. Among the various items mentioned in her will, we find some relating to our own land. Diocese of Ohio, £200. Books for Ohio, £50. Newfoundland schools, £100. Also Barley Wood school, Ceylon, £100. Distressed Vaudois. £180. After an enumeration of seventy-one objects, to which fifty thousand dollars were appropriated, the remainder of her property was to be invested in three per cent. consols, to increase the endowment of the new church of St. Philip and Jacob, which began to be erected in one of the destitute parishes of Bristol, numbering a population of sixteen thousand souls, hitherto without the public services of the gospel. It was now suggested adding a school to the church, which should bear her name, and thus commemorate her memory through an instrumentality which she had used with such eminent success—*teaching the poor.* At a meeting holden in Clifton on the October following, these resolutions were presented and adopted:

"That the distinguished talents and qualifications of the late Miss Hannah More, consecrated most usefully and efficiently, throughout the course of a long life, to the noblest ends of Christian benevolence, have justly embalmed her memory in the public esteem and veneration.

"That this meeting is of opinion it is desirable to convey to posterity some public memorial of the sentiments embodied in the preceding resolution.

"That a subscription be entered into for placing a tablet to the memory of Miss Hannah More, in the parish church of Wrington, where her own remains and those of her four sisters are interred; and should the sum collected exceed what may be deemed necessary for the proper execution of such purpose, that the surplus be devoted to the establishment of a school—to bear her name—in connection with the new church in the parish of St. Philip and Jacob in Bristol, towards the endowment of which she has bequeathed the residue of her estate."

Six thousand dollars remained after the erection of the tablet, costing six hundred dollars, which may be seen in the parish church at Wrington, bearing this humble testimony to her worth and genius:

Sacred to the Memory

OF

HANNAH MORE.

SHE WAS BORN IN THE PARISH OF STAPLETON, NEAR BRISTOL, A. D. 1745, AND DIED AT CLIFTON, SEPTEMBER 7TH, A. D. 1833.

ENDOWED WITH GREAT INTELLECTUAL POWERS,
AND EARLY DISTINGUISHED BY THE SUCCESS
OF HER LITERARY LABORS,
SHE ENTERED THE WORLD UNDER CIRCUMSTANCES
TENDING TO FIX HER AFFECTIONS ON ITS VANITIES;
BUT, INSTRUCTED IN THE SCHOOL OF CHRIST
TO FORM A JUST ESTIMATE OF THE REAL END OF HUMAN EXISTENCE,
SHE CHOSE THE BETTER PART,
AND CONSECRATED HER TIME AND TALENTS
TO THE GLORY OF GOD AND THE GOOD OF HER FELLOW-CREATURES,
IN A LIFE OF PRACTICAL PIETY AND DIFFUSIVE BENEFICENCE.

HER NUMEROUS WRITINGS IN SUPPORT OF RELIGION AND ORDER,
AT A CRISIS WHEN BOTH WERE RUDELY ASSAILED,
WERE EQUALLY EDIFYING TO THE READERS OF ALL CLASSES,
AT ONCE DELIGHTING THE WISE,
AND INSTRUCTING THE IGNORANT AND SIMPLE.

IN THE EIGHTY-NINTH YEAR OF HER AGE,
BELOVED BY HER FRIENDS, AND VENERATED BY THE PUBLIC,
SHE CLOSED HER CAREER OF USEFULNESS
IN HUMBLE RELIANCE ON THE MERCIES OF GOD,
THROUGH FAITH IN THE MERITS OF HER REDEEMER.

HER MORTAL REMAINS ARE DEPOSITED IN A VAULT IN THIS CHURCHYARD, WHICH ALSO CONTAINS THOSE OF HER FOUR SISTERS, WHO RESIDED WITH HER AT BARLEY WOOD, IN THIS PARISH, HER FAVORITE ABODE, AND WHO ACTIVELY COÖPERATED IN HER UNWEARIED ACTS OF CHRISTIAN BENEVOLENCE.

CONCLUSION.

We have played with her at Stapleton, studied with her at Bristol, admired her at London; we have gone with her to the thoughtful retirement of Cowslip Green, joined the sisterhood at Barley Wood, visited her schools, heard her conversation, beheld her popularity, witnessed her daily life; and now, shall we pass from the contemplation of a character like hers no wiser or better than before? Are there no lessons of *self-application* in this brief sketch? What shall the young of our own day learn from the light of her shining example?

Much of the personal influence which Hannah More exercised in the brilliant circles of literary life was undoubtedly owing to her unrivalled powers of conversation, full of wit, sense, and originality; to these were added a penetrating and sagacious mind, which, with its thorough knowledge of mankind, obtained by a large acquaintance with almost every class of society, enabled her to comprehend the dangers to which the English masses were exposed, from the sophistries of French infidelity and English demagogues, and instantly to seize and apply an appropriate remedy. Her tracts and stories for the times are among her most remarkable productions, displaying as they do the nicest perceptions of character and opinion; they silenced the murmurs of discontent and the doubts of skepticism, and were like oil upon the rising waves of revolution.

Her first works upon the irreligious habits and tendencies of the higher classes in English society were characterized by clear and candid statements of the most obvious and reasonable requirements of Christianity—statements uttered with such discretion and truthfulness, that their directness could not offend, even where it was least welcome. They were read and pondered.

As she herself came to clearer and fuller apprehensions of truth and duty, the nature and importance of her mission became more distinctly revealed: then followed that series of religious teaching, that plain and faithful application of the principles of the gospel to the heart and life, which tended so powerfully to quicken the spiritual life of the church and elevate the standard of practical piety. Miss More felt the moral want of her times: these were general declension and coldness in the religious world; customs and maxims had insensibly stolen upon the church, which sullied its purity and diminished its influence. The writings of Wilberforce and Hannah More, warmed and enriched by a living faith, infused new life into dead forms, and gave to the Christian profession a quickened conscience, higher aims, and a holier life.

The intellectual gifts which distinguished Hannah More, rich and influential as they were, formed not her chief excellence, nor that perhaps which most commends itself to our reverence and affection. It was her *solid and earnest piety* which imparted breadth and depth, strength and beauty to her character, and made her influence felt even to the ends of the earth. Herein is that with which we have to do. What were the elements of that faith which obtained so good a report, and left so shining an example?

There is a religion of taste, which admires the beauties of this world, and is awed by the grandeur of its Maker. It is inspired more by the book of nature than of revelation—more by the natural than the moral attributes of God; it seeks solitary places, and dies amid the din and bustle of noon-day life; it shrinks from the sin and distress of the actual, and sighs for the good and beautiful of the ideal; it yearns for the dim aisles of an old past, and would seek the aid of painter and sculptor to help it in its devotions; it is amiable, tasteful, and full of reverence. Was it the religion of taste which moulded a character like Hannah More's?

"I am a passionate admirer of whatever is beautiful in nature or exquisite in art," she declares. "These are the gifts of God, but no part of his essence; they proceed from God's goodness, and should kindle our gratitude to him; but I cannot conceive that the most enchanting beauties of nature, or the most splendid productions of the fine arts, have any necessary connection with religion. You will observe that I mean the religion of Christ, not that of Plato; the religion of reality, and not that of the beau ideal.

"Adam sinned in a garden too beautiful for us to have any conception of it. The Israelites selected fair groves and pleasant mountains for the peculiar scenes of their idolatry. The most exquisite pictures and statues have been produced in those parts of Europe where pure religion has made the least progress. These decorate religion, but they neither produce nor advance it. They are the enjoyments and refreshments of life, and very compatible with true religion, but they make no part of it. Athens was at once the most learned and the most polished city in the world; so devoted to the fine arts, that it is said to have contained more statues than men; yet in this eloquent city the eloquent apostle's preaching made but one proselyte in the whole areopagus.

"Nothing, it appears to me, can essentially improve the character and benefit society, but a saving knowledge of the distinctive doctrines of Christianity. I mean a deep and abiding sense in the heart, of our fallen nature, of our actual and personal sinfulness, of our lost state but for the redemption wrought for us by Jesus Christ, and of our universal necessity, and the conviction that this change alone can be effected by the influence of the Holy Spirit. This is not a splendid, but it is a saving religion; it is humbling now, that it may be elevating hereafter. It appears to me also, that the requisition which the Christian religion makes of the most highly gifted, as well as of the most meanly endowed, is, that after the loftiest and most successful exercise of the most brilliant talents, the favored possessor should lay his talents and himself at the foot of the cross, with the same deep self-abasement and self-renunciation as his more illiterate neighbor, and this from a conviction of who it is that hath made them to differ."

Again, there is a fashionable religion, priding itself upon orthodox doctrines, but lax enough in orthodox practice: it is trifling, irresponsible, and florid, mixed up with frivolity and worldliness; enjoyment is the measure of duty; it seeks to be pleased, not instructed, and in the pursuit has contracted habits which have proved fatal snares, and imbibed tastes which have weakened and debased its principles. How is it rebuked by the strong language of earnest piety and a living faith!

"We must avoid," says Hannah More, "as much as in us lies, all *such society*, all *such amusements*, all *such tempers* which it is the daily business of a Christian to subdue, and all those feelings which it is his constant duty to suppress. Some things, which are apparently innocent and do not assume an alarming aspect or bear a dangerous character—things which the generality of decorous people affirm (how truly we know not) to be safe for them; yet if we find that these things stir up in us improper propensities—if they awaken thoughts which ought not to be excited—if they abate our love for religious exercises, or infringe on our time for performing them—if they make spiritual concerns appear insipid—if they wind our heart a little more about the world—in short, if we have formerly found them injurious to our own souls, then let no example or persuasion, no belief of their alleged innocence, no plea of their perfect safety tempt us to indulge in them. It matters little to *our* security what they are to others. Our business is with ourselves. Our responsibility is on our own heads. Others cannot know the side on which we are assailable. Let our own unbiassed judgment determine our opinion, let our own experience decide for our own conduct.

"As our kind of reading has much to do with the formation of our religious character, and the fostering of corrupt or correct tastes, we cannot forbear noticing that very prevalent sort of reading which is little less productive of evil, little less prejudicial to moral and mental improvement, than that which carries a more formidable appearance. We cannot confine our censure to those more corrupt writings which deprave the heart, debauch the imagination, and poison the principles. Of these the turpitude is so obvious, that no caution on this head, it is presumed, *can* be necessary. But if justice forbids us to confound the insipid with the mischievous, the idle with the vicious, and the frivolous with the profligate, still we can only admit of shades, deep shades we allow, of difference. These works, if comparatively harmless, yet debase the taste, slacken the intellectual nerve, let down the understanding, set the fancy loose, and send it gadding among low and mean objects. They not only run away with the time which should be given to better things, but gradually destroy all taste for better things. They sink the mind to their own standard, and give it a sluggish reluctance, we had almost said a moral incapacity for every thing above their level. The mind, by long habit of stooping, loses its erectness, and yields to its degradation. It becomes so low and narrow by the littleness of the things which engage it, that it requires a painful effort to lift itself high enough, or to open itself wide enough to embrace great and noble objects. The appetite is vitiated. Excess, instead of producing a surfeit, by weakening the digestion only induces a loathing for stronger nourishment. The faculties which might have been expanding in works of science, or soaring in the contemplation of genius, become satisfied with the impertinences of the most ordinary fiction, lose their relish for the severity of truth, the elegance of taste, and the soberness of religion. Lulled in the torpor of repose, the intellect dozes, and enjoys in its waking dream,

"All the wild trash of sleep, without the rest.

"In avoiding books which excite the passions, it would seem strange to include even some devotional works. Yet such as merely kindle warm feelings are not always the safest. Let us rather prefer those which, while they tend to raise a devotional spirit, awaken the affections without disordering them; which while they elevate the desires, purify them; which show us our own nature, and lay open its corruptions: such as show us the malignity of sin, the deceitfulness of our hearts, the feebleness of our best resolutions; such as teach us to pull off the mask from the fairest appearances, and discover every hiding-place where some lurking evil would conceal itself; such as show us not what we appear to others, but what we really are; such as, coöperating with our interior feelings and showing us our natural state, point out our absolute need of a Redeemer, lead us to seek to him for pardon from a conviction that there is no other refuge, no other salvation. Let us be conversant with such writings as teach us that, while we long to obtain the remission of our transgressions, we must not desire the remission of our duties."

"A life devoted to trifles," she again says, "not only takes away the inclination, but the capacity for higher pursuits. The truths of Christianity have scarcely more influence on a frivolous than on a profligate character. If the mind be so absorbed, not merely with what is vicious, but with what is useless, as to be thoroughly disinclined to the activities of a life of piety, it matters little what the cause is which so disinclines it. If these habits cannot be accused of great moral evil, yet it argues a low state of mind, that a being who has an eternity at stake, can abandon itself to trivial pursuits. If the great concern of life cannot be secured without habitual watchfulness, how is it to be secured by habitual carelessness? It will afford little comfort to the trifler, when at the last reckoning he gives in his long negative catalogue, that the more ostensible offender was worse employed. The trifler will not be weighed in the scale with the profligate, but in the balance of the sanctuary."

Are there not many who may well take heed? Shall we be content with the "beggarly elements" of a religious profession, when God demands a holy life?

Still further, earnest piety prevents that *skepticism* which is liable to creep into the soul at a certain stage in the religious experience, and which, if not expelled, chills our faith, until we have only a name to live. Have you not known many who entered upon the religious life with the fairest promise? How lovely were the first blossoms of piety; what prayers were offered for their fruit—what hopes were entertained of their usefulness! Time elapses, and alas, how is the fine gold become dim! They have lost their confidence; they see *no use* in that wherein they once delighted; their love is cold, their faith low, their hands feeble; they are weary, discouraged, faint-hearted.

Why is this so? Amid the first exercises of the renewed soul, ah, there was no account laid with remaining corruptions within, and discouragements and trial from without. What various hinderances beset the way; what disappointments chill the heart; what sins still clog the soul! They may have learned to labor, but not to *wait:* while planting the seed, they looked for the harvest. This forms the great crisis in the religious life, when in the waning light of our first love to God, we first fully comprehend all which that love demands—when the *ardor of feeling* is to be replaced by the *steadfastness* of principle—when the life that has been given us, no longer dependent upon the nurture of Christian friends, must henceforth depend upon ourselves: *our* watchfulness, *our* labors, *our* care must nourish it, strengthen it, and bring it to the stature of a perfect man in Christ Jesus. From this day of labor and of trial, alas, how many shrink! Who is sufficient for these things? cries the fainting believer.

"I can do all things through Christ which strengtheneth me," responds a living faith, which bears the soul through its doubts and fears, and teaches that hardest, last learned lesson, yet best of all, that in yielding *a willing obedience to God, and striving to do his work, he will work in us* both to will and to do of his own good pleasure—Christ in man.

This is the substance of an earnest piety—of a working, saving, living faith, beautifully and impressively illustrated in the life and labors of Hannah More.

Who is striving after it? Who will go and do likewise?

Interesting and Valuable Biographies.

Life of Rev. Justin Edwards, D. D.

Constrained by the love of Christ, he devoted a long life to the ministry, and the efficient promotion of the cause of Temperance, the Sabbath, and the study of the Bible. Steel portrait. 556 pp. 12mo.

Memoir of Rev. James Milnor, D. D.

By Rev. JOHN S. STONE, D. D., with an admirable likeness. Full of incident and instruction, alike attractive to the ardent youth, the man of business, the humble Christian, and the mature Theologian. 549 pp. 12mo.

Life of George Whitefield.

With steel portrait, and other engravings. His brilliant career is traced as he preached eighteen thousand sermons, crossed the ocean thirteen times, and poured evangelical light on millions of minds in Great Britain and the United States. 514 pp. 12mo.

Life of Rev. Dr. Scott, the Commentator

Steel portrait. Rising from obscurity by his own energy, he became preëminently useful in the pulpit and through the press. 502 pp. 12mo.

Life, Character, and Writings of Dr. Philip Doddridge.

With steel portrait. Prepared with great care and research, and has a value beyond that of any mere biography. 480 pp. 12mo.

Memoir of Rev. Jeremiah Hallock.

With sketch of Rev. Moses Hallock. Faithful and successful pastors, and laborers in the great revivals early in the present century. Steel frontispiece. 389 pp. 12mo.

Memoir of Rev. John Summerfield.

Steel portrait. Few memoirs are more entertaining, or richer in the attractions of the cross, or more worthy of a world-wide circulation. 339 pp. 12mo.

Life of Rev. Philip Henry.

Father of the Commentator. One of the richest memoirs in our language. Steel portrait. 346 pp. 12mo.

Memoir of Rev. Matthew Henry,

The great Commentator. In his youth he visited Baxter in prison, and drank deeply of his spirit. 218 pp. 18mo.

The Haldanes and their Friends.

A narrative of deepest interest, describing the labors of the devoted brothers Robert and James Alexander Haldane, with their contemporaries, in the glorious revival about the beginning of the present century. Steel portrait. 278 pp. 12mo.

Life of Rev. Richard Knill,

Of St. Petersburg, Russia. Steel portrait. He was owned of God in leading very many souls to Jesus, scores of whom became preachers of the gospel. 358 pp. 18mo.

Memoir of Rev. Dr. Payson.

With portrait. It opens before the reader a rich fountain of Christian experience, and presents impressive and beautiful illustrations of truth and duty. 486 pp. 18mo.

Memoir of James B. Taylor.

With portrait. A character of uncommon attractions to old and young. 528 pp. 18mo.

Life of David Brainerd.

New edition, with enlarged type, and engravings. Uniting in a remarkable manner the fervor of personal piety and devoted missionary zeal. 482 pp. 18mo.

Life of Harlan Page.

Steel portrait. The power of his example is seen at this day in greatly increased personal effort for the conversion of souls to Christ. 243 pp. 18mo.

Memoir of Rev. John Newton.

A most striking narrative. The latter years of his life endeared his memory to millions. 254 pp. 18mo.

Memoir of Charles H. Porter.

Kindred in spirit to Harlan Page and James B. Taylor. 168 pp. 18mo.

Life of Richard Baxter.

Presenting his own interesting history, and also the rude and persecuting spirit of the times. 181 pp. 18mo.

Life of Normand Smith.

The Christian serving God in his business. 72 pp. 18mo.

History and Narratives.

D'Aubigne's History of the Great Reformation.

In five volumes 12mo; 2,494 pp. Five steel portraits. A learned professor has well said, this is "one of the most timely and useful works of the present century. The style is graphic and full of life, and a delightful spirit of evangelical piety pervades the whole."

Sketches from Life. Series I. and II.

These two volumes comprise more than three hundred and fifty interesting and impressive narratives, with many engravings. 12mo.

Revival Sketches and Manual.

By Rev. Dr. Humphrey. A work adapted to encourage Christians in efforts to promote the cause of Christ. 476 pp. 12mo.

Elegant Narratives.

Twenty-four select tracts, beautifully printed and illustrated. 500 pp. 12mo.

Pictorial Narratives.

Twenty-four illustrated tracts. 252 pp. 12mo.

Anecdotes for the Family Circle.

Containing three hundred and eight anecdotes, each conveying some valuable lesson, full of interest and instruction to all. Finely illustrated. 503 pp. 18mo.

Haste to the Rescue.

A narrative of God's blessing upon the noble efforts of an English lady to reclaim and lead to Christ the laboring classes of a large town. With frontispiece. 324 pp. 18mo.

Seamen's Narratives.

An interesting volume for sailors. Illustrated. 284 pp. 18mo.

Annals of the Poor.

Legh Richmond's beautiful narratives of the Dairyman's Daughter, African Servant, and Young Cottager. 320 pp. 18mo.

The Dairyman's Daughter.

New edition, illustrated, large type. 180 pp. 18mo.

The Young Cottager.

In the same style as the above. 143 pp.

HELPS TO BIBLE STUDY.

The Family Bible, Royal Octavo, Revised Edition.

With brief Notes and Instructions, Marginal References, an Introduction to each book, a Harmony of the Gospels, new Maps, Tables of Patriarchs, Prophets, and Apostles, Bible Chronology, and a Family Record. For general use in family worship and Bible study. 1,504 pages. In one volume sheep, or three volumes cloth.

Family Testament and Psalms,

With Notes, etc. A beautiful volume of 524 pages super-royal 8vo.

Pocket Testament,

With Notes, Maps, etc. 18mo, 810 pages.

A Dictionary of the Holy Bible,

For general use in the study of the Scriptures, with five Maps, Chronological and other Tables, and two hundred and fifty Engravings. 534 pages, large 12mo.

Bible Atlas and Gazetteer,

Royal octavo, 32 pages, with six fine maps, a list of all the geographical names in Scripture, and valuable Tables.

Cruden's Condensed Concordance.

A fine edition. 561 pages, 8vo.

Locke's Commonplace-Book to the Holy Bible.

412 pages 8vo.

The Bible Text-Book,

Or the principal Texts relating to the Persons, Places, and Subjects occurring in the Holy Scriptures. Colored Maps, and Tables. 280 pages, 18mo.

Youth's Bible Studies,

Complete in six parts. Part I. The Pentateuch. II. Historical Books. III. The Prophets. IV. Poetical Books. V. The Gospels. VI. The Acts, Epistles, etc. In a set with case.

Gallaudet's Youth's Scripture Biography,

Complete in eleven volumes. 49 Engravings. In a case.

www.ingramcontent.com/pod-product-compliance
Lightning Source LLC
LaVergne TN
LVHW010219110826
845151LV00004B/1138

* 9 7 8 1 4 2 5 5 2 6 5 7 3 *